Dealing with difference

Teresa Williams and Adrian Green

Dealing with difference

How trainers can take account of cultural diversity

Gower

Published by
Gower Publishing
Gower House
Croft Road
Aldershot
Hampshire GU11 3HR
England

Gower
Old Post Road
Brookfield
Vermont 05036
USA

British Library Cataloguing in Publication Data
Williams, Teresa
Dealing with Difference: How Trainers Can
Take Account of Cultural Diversity
I. Title II. Green, Adrian
658.3
ISBN 0-566-07425-7

Library of Congress Cataloging-in-Publication Data
Williams, Teresa,
   Dealing with difference: how trainers can take account of cultural diversity/
Teresa Williams and Adrian Green.
      p. cm.
   Includes bibliographical references and index.
   ISBN 0–566–07425–7
   1. Employees – Training of – Social aspects. 2. Multiculturalism.
3. Employee training personnel – Training of. I. Green, Adrian.
II. Title.
HF5549.5.T7W492   1993
658.3'1245–dc20   93–36859
                                                                CIP

Typeset in 11 point Times by Poole Typesetting (Wessex) Limited and printed in Great Britain at the University Press, Cambridge.

Contents

Part II Learners from different cultural groups

Part III Culture and the learning event

Part IV The way forward

Preface

This book is aimed at all who are involved with helping others to learn and develop. It will help them identify ways to take into account the implications of culture when trying to achieve better quality learning and transfer of learning to the workplace.

Our work has been based on a wide range of experiences, theories and ideas from the UK and abroad. We have concentrated on taking a practical approach to the subject.

We would like to thank all those who have spent time with us sharing their ideas, experiences, assumptions, values and beliefs in relation to the process of learning and development. In particular we would like to thank Norman Eccles for his support and encouragement, Steve Williams for his technical and moral support throughout, and Peter and Amanda Green for their patience and understanding.

Teresa Williams
Adrian Green

List of illustrations

Tables

Diagrams

List of activities for trainers

List of activities for learners

Part I — Culture and training

1 | Introduction

This book is about enabling learning by taking the implications of culture on the learning and development process into account. Cultural values are usually fundamental to our way of thinking, to the learner's way of thinking and to the way we do things in an organisation. Yet in the learning process culture is often neglected . It can be the vital link between the learners, the learning content and transfer of learning into the workplace.

Each participant in the learning process faces different problems at different stages. Typical questions are:

Trainer
Q How can I be more effective in the way I help people with the learning and development process?
Senior management
Q How can we get better return on investment on learning and development?
Learner
Q How can I get help and ideas I can use back at work?
Q Will the learning event meet my needs?
Learner's manager
Q Will the learning event make a difference to the learner when they return to work?

You may well find that achieving satisfaction in one area will create dissatisfaction in one or more of the other areas. Sometimes the needs of the various players appear to be mutually exclusive. This book demonstrates how to use culture as a tool to help with these differing demands on us as trainers.

The book is about the implications of culture on the learning and development process. It is designed to give the trainer a number of concepts and ideas together with many practical exercises which can be used to take the implications of culture into account. We provide ideas and options to consider rather than precise instructions about what to do. This is because the cultures in which each of you have to operate will be different.

To avoid confusion the following terminology has been used throughout this book. The term 'trainer' denotes the trainer, tutor, teacher or facilitator who is guiding the learning process. The term 'learner' is used to denote the learner, trainee, student, course member or course participant. The term 'boss' has been used to denote the person who is responsible for the learner in terms of identifying training needs, giving support on the job, briefing and debriefing the learner and so on. (In some cases different people may be responsible for these different functions.) We also acknowledge that it may be a manager, a supervisor, team leader, senior clerk or specialist who is given this role.

A definition of culture

There are many definitions of culture, and some of these are explored later in the book, but for our present purpose the working definition of culture is:

> 'meanings, beliefs, understandings, values and assumptions subscribed to by a group of people.'

Scope of the book

This book does not attempt to give advice and guidance on specific national cultures as there are other sources of information on that subject. Instead of stereotyping and classifying people, we offer ideas and concepts which can be applied in a wide range of situations, particularly those in which initially you do not know much about the learner's culture. The book aims to both raise awareness and furnish some practical ways of helping learners and trainers.

The ideas in this book can give you new ways of tackling common problems that occur with learners. For instance, learners may:
- Become 'sick' rather than attend the learning event.
- Be too busy for training.
- Have to return to work to deal with a 'crisis'.
- Experience poor transfer of learning to work.
- Have a low perception of the relevance of material covered in sessions.

- Become withdrawn or obstructive with the group.
- Say 'It won't work in my department.'

Taking cultural implications into account will not solve all learning and development problems. Consider it as one of a number of important factors to respond to when you are trying to make the most effective use of time and other resources during the learning and development process.

Learning outcomes

The material in this book will help you to:

- Modify and design learning events that take account of each learner's culture.
- Reduce prejudice and stereotyping about learners.
- Run learning events that do not force learners to compromise the culture they subscribe to (though you may decide to challenge their values and assumptions in a positive and constructive way).
- Achieve a better return on investment of the money and time spent on learning by working with the prevailing culture rather than ignoring it and inadvertently working against it.

Why worry about culture?

A mismatch between the learner's culture at work and the culture of the trainers and/or other learners can lead to:

- Ineffective learning during a programme.
- Ineffective transfer of learning back to work.
- Longer term loss of credibility, respect and, therefore, effectiveness for those leading or facilitating the learning process.

With increasing cultural diversity now a feature of many organisations, more and more trainers will need to manage the implications of more than one culture during learning and development. For example, within an organisation there may be differences in culture in work groups or teams, departments, branches, regions, levels of the hierarchy, occupational groups, different countries, ethnic groups or national groups. Diagram 1 shows some of the many cultural groupings of which learners can be a part.

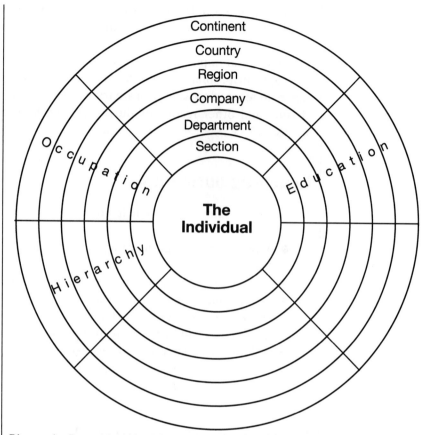

Continent
Country
Region
Company
Department
Section

Occupation

Education

**The
Individual**

Hierarchy

Diagram 1. Recognising cultural issues becomes more important to the learning process as cultural diversity increases.

There are many factors which are increasing, and will continue to increase, cultural diversity. They include:

- More rapid organisational change. As industries and organisations change, fewer people are employed in the same organisation – or even field of work – for their entire working lives.
- Increasing free movement of labour across countries.
- Changing demographic trends which force employers to extend their search to meet skill shortages.
- Relocation of organisations. As organisations move to cheaper or more attractive locations not all their employees relocate too. Organisations usually recruit some staff from the new location and keep some staff from the old location – an inevitable mix of culture.
- Changes in legislation. Laws relating to sex discrimination, race discrimination, equal opportunities and movement of labour will all lead to increasing diversity of people employed.

6

- Technological changes such as improved transport. This means that people are more prepared to commute and have a wider choice of employment. Changing jobs becomes more feasible.

So increasingly, when learners either individually or in groups and their trainers come together there is a diversity of cultures. This means there is an increasing chance of differences in the beliefs, understanding, values and underlying assumptions which those people are bringing to the learning event.

You can increase the effectiveness of the time that is spent on learning and development by taking culture into account. To do this you need to be able to:

- Identify how culture can influence the learning and development process.
- Recognise the main features of both your own culture and the learner's culture.
- Identify the way cultural differences in a group of learners can affect learning.
- Show how cultural differences between the trainer and learner can affect learning.
- Take these cultural differences into account when planning, developing or delivering learning strategies and methodologies.

By recognising learner culture you can help learners to:

- Settle down more quickly with the other learners in their group.
- Learn from and help other learners in their group.
- Identify which ideas can be transferred effectively to their workplace.
- Discover alternative approaches which may be more suitable to the situations they face.
- Adapt and modify suggestions, theories and models to take account of the culture in which they are working.
- Explain, discuss and analyse issues which they see as being important because of the values and beliefs held by them or the people with whom they work.

So by understanding the implications of culture on the learning and development process you can help the learner not only to settle into the learning process more quickly but also to learn at a faster rate, and to apply the learning more effectively.

Understanding a learner's culture

Let's look now at what understanding a learner's culture means in practice. Basically it involves recognising the following:

- How they see, think and feel about things – and why.
- How they express what they see, think and feel.
- How this differs from your (trainer) culture and from other cultures they may have to relate to.
- How they solve problems, both as individuals and as a group (which will of course be based on their assumptions, values and beliefs).

Before you can do any of these things you need to understand your own culture: your own values, beliefs and assumptions. Most of us are not even aware of our basic assumptions. We are not usually trained to explore them. However, before you can understand and work with other cultures effectively and consciously, you need to understand your own culture more fully. Many of the activities in this book will help you to make a start.

Risks of ignoring cultural issues

The composition of the work force today is much less traditional than it was. Situations where people in a job were of the same sex, of a similar educational level or background, from the same town or community, of the same first language, employed in the same type of work for the whole of their working lives, are considerably fewer.

So the risks of not addressing cultural issues are increasing. Some of the main risks in a learning situation are that:

- Stereotyping is reinforced.
- Increasing intolerance may build up in the group.
- Misunderstandings increase.
- Frustrations can become intolerable.
- Learners or trainers may switch off.
- Defensiveness increases.
- Blocking, criticising or attacking behaviours can increase.
- Learners withdraw from the learning process – either physically or mentally.

Options

When there are significant cultural differences you and your learners have a number of options. Either or both of you can choose to:

- Ignore the differences.
- Attempt to change.
- Attempt to avoid the differences.
- Manage the differences.

We are not implying that any of these options are right or wrong, merely that you need to be conscious of them and their implications, and understand how culture relates to the effectiveness of the learning process.

Let's explore these options in a little more detail. The following examples are of the actions trainers and learners sometimes take because of cultural differences (culture is not of course the only factor involved).

Ignore the differences

One option is to treat everyone in the same way based on your assumptions or stereotyping of the group. You can work to a prepared approach, delivering a standard or even off-the-shelf product. It may be that you believe that a particular approach is best and decide that it is not appropriate to explore whether or not it is based on values and beliefs shared by the learners. This approach can help you to save design time, means that you and other trainers can prepare ahead of time and have a number of options at hand. It can also suit a more structured approach.

A recent example of ignoring the differences comes from a colleague who was attending a course designed and delivered by an American company to a British audience. Over two days a substantial amount of the material was delivered via videos showing an American expert. The learners asked for more of the delivery to be given by the trainer live as they found it difficult to watch so many videos. The trainer was very reluctant to do this believing it would dilute the material – nobody else would be as good as the American expert on the video – which would compromise the quality of the training. It was the American company's belief that training should be of the same quality and that everyone should benefit from the delivery by the American expert (even though this was by video).

On a more positive note, an example of training that is not specially tailored but is nevertheless very successful comes from the world of computer-based training. Off-the-shelf packages come in a standard format. The design is the same regardless of who buys them. The success is in the choosing. If you can choose a standard package that happens to

9

suit a number of trainees then you can have a very cost effective approach. Problems will occur, however, if you insist on using it for all trainees with that training need rather than selecting the method which suits each individual. So this is an example of where you ignore differences when designing but take differences into account when selecting the training.

Either you or the learner attempts to change

Sometimes either you or the learner tries to operate as though you subscribe to the other's culture. This often happens to learners when they attend a training programme, especially a residential one away from their organisation's premises.

The learners attempt to belong to the training culture that is usually set by the trainer. In many cases learners find it a comfortable, acceptable culture in which to work for the duration of the programme. At the end there may well be a sense of euphoria and strong group identity and feelings. This often leads to a sense of disappointment that the group now has to separate and a feeling of loss when they go back to work. As a result they experience difficulties when they return to their workplace. This is because many learners try to operate in the same way as they did on the programme (or wish they could) and find that it does not work. The culture is different – the values, assumptions, beliefs are different. Learners often then experience frustration because 'it doesn't work in my section': 'the training was a lot of fun, and a good experience, but it doesn't fit with reality.'

On the other hand trying to change to fit the other person's culture can be beneficial. It can be useful in gaining a first-hand insight into a different way of doing things. It can help to unlock barriers caused by lack of experience of different ways of doing things.

Attempt to avoid the differences

There are a number of ways in which trainers, either consciously or unconsciously, try to avoid cultural differences. For example:

- Some trainers avoid training certain groups and rationalise their decision by saying that:
  - Those learners' needs are of lower priority.
  - It is not a worthwhile investment because those people cannot be bothered to learn.
  - Those people are unlikely to be promoted.
  Sometimes it is done by:

- Just quietly ignoring those people.
- Saying that you will do it next year.
- 'Delegating' that area to a colleague or subordinate.
- Buying in someone to do it for you.

● Avoidance can also be achieved by careful groupings on learning events. Consciously or unconsciously trainers and learners
are sometimes grouped so as to avoid particular differences in
beliefs and values.

● Placing the learner on an external learning event and bringing in
an external trainer are other ways of avoiding cultural differences. Often trainers place a person or group on an external
course because to include them on an in-house programme
would 'rock the boat'; 'they would not fit in'.

Typical actions which learners take to avoid cultural differences
include:

● Adopting withdrawn and retiring behaviour. The learner finds
that others have different views based on different values and
beliefs. Learners either do not feel confident enough to challenge or explain their viewpoint, or feel threatened. Their
defence is silence and they mentally withdraw from the programme, doing just enough to be socially acceptable.

● Physically withdrawing from a course. This can be achieved by
claiming sickness; having a domestic or work crisis; by simply
not attending; or by going back to work on the grounds that the
course was a mistake or that it was not relevant.

● Asking to attend an external programme away from colleagues
in preference to an in-house one. Sometimes learners sense that
the culture in which they operate is different and do not want to
be challenged or threatened by attending an internal programme
with colleagues they know. They may feel that they will not be
able to deal with the culture differences and that to challenge
other people's ideas on an internal programme will somehow
affect their working relationship in the future.

Some plausible reasons given for attending an external learning event
or avoiding an internal event include:

- Not being available for any of the in-house dates.
- Asking for the opportunity to get ideas from learners who work
for other organisations.
- Claiming that they need a particular optional module which is
not offered in-house.

You will need to check whether these reasons are genuine or whether they are just excuses to justify a learner's attendance at an external programme and so avoid discussing issues with colleagues who have different opinions.

Avoiding differences is not always a bad thing. If your goal is to help someone to learn a particular topic or skill, then the most cost effective way might be to take avoidance action and place them with another trainer, or on another programme. Being realistic, we may not have the time, energy or emotional strength to develop ourselves so that we can deal with all situations.

Manage the differences

There are many ways in which trainers and learners can manage cultural differences in a positive and effective way. This book concentrates on those ways and the following material is designed to help you develop that approach.

The trainer's role

Culture influences what you see as being new, different, significant or obvious. If the learner is of a different culture there may be some inherent differences in your views and values. You may need to establish some common ground, or, in some cases, decide to try to understand and work with the learner's culture and perceptions.

Your culture will affect:

- How you behave with others.
- Your attitudes towards them.
- How you communicate.
- How you exert control.
- How you guide the learning process (or not!).

The trainer needs to know enough about the learner's culture to be able to make an informed choice rather than guess or stereotype. The learner needs to be able to relate to the help which you are offering. There are many factors which affect the learning process and Diagram 2 shows some of the influences of culture on that process.

There is more and more pressure today to help meet individual learning and development needs in a way that is tailored to the learner. In many areas learners already believe that a quality approach is one that is geared directly to their needs in a way that suits their learning style. By taking culture into account you will be better able to provide that quality of service.

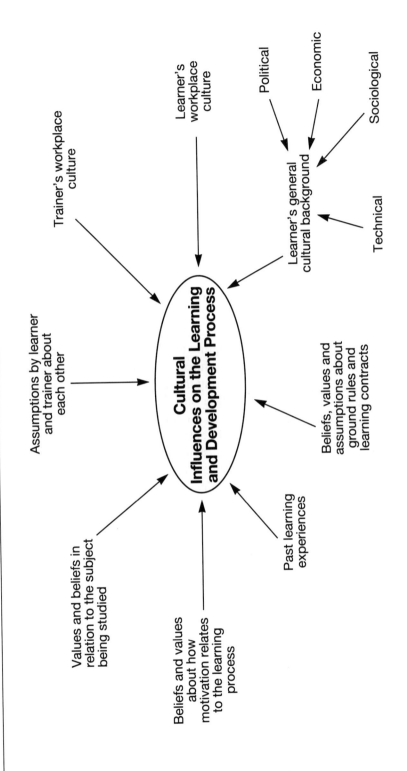

13   **Diagram 2.** Cultural influences on the learning and development process

Summary

- Recognising and managing cultural differences can help to achieve:
  - More effective learning on a learning event.
  - Improved transfer of learning back to the workplace.
- Diversity of culture is an issue which more and more trainers are facing because of changes in:
  - Organisational structure and location.
  - Legislation.
  - Workers' expectations and needs.
  - Movement of labour.
  - Technology and transport.
  - Demography.
  - Skills and expertise required.
- Where there are significant cultural differences, the options include:
  - Ignoring the differences.
  - Attempting to adapt to the other person's culture.
  - Attempting to avoid the differences.
  - Managing the differences.
- To increase the effectiveness of the learning process by taking culture into account you need to be able to:
  - Identify how culture can influence the learning process.
  - Recognise the main features of your own culture.
  - Take these cultural differences into account when planning, developing or delivering learning events.

2 | What is culture?

The working definition of culture proposed in Chapter 1 was 'meanings, beliefs, understandings, values and assumptions subscribed to by a group of people'. The group of people may all belong to an organisation, a clan, a nation, an occupation, a department, section or team.

The term culture is used to describe the way in which people live and survive – ways of acting, thinking, feeling, doing. It gives guidance on how to respond in times of uncertainty or ambiguity. It is learned rather than innate. Culture is often strongest where a group of people need a lot of reassurance, or where they are less willing or able to tolerate uncertainty or ambiguity.

There are many other definitions of culture and it is useful to look at some of them to see the similarities and differences. For example, Edgar Schein (1984) sees culture as 'that pattern of basic assumptions that a given group has invented, discovered or developed in learning to cope with its problems of external adaptation and internal integration, that has worked well enough to be considered valid, and therefore, to be taught to new members as the correct way to perceive, think, and feel in relation to these problems.'

According to Michael Armstrong (1989) 'Corporate culture encompasses the norms and core values of an enterprise and manifests itself in the form of organisational climates, management style, organisation behaviour, or "the way things are done around here", and the structure and systems of the organisation.'

Implications for the trainer

As a trainer it is important to recognise the corporate culture and the learner's culture. What are the differences? How do they compare with the culture in which you like to operate? If learners are experiencing uncertainty, threat, fear or change they are likely to cling to their culture and to ways of behaving supported by that culture.

If the training which you propose conforms to the learner's culture then it is likely to be more readily received. If, however, the training encourages people to break from their culture in some way then the change process can be much longer and more difficult. It may result in only temporary change taking place because people may feel that the need to conform and be a full member of their old cultural grouping is more important than improving productivity or using more effective work methods.

If their training is to be effective in the long term, trainers need to recognise these issues and to deal with them.

An example of what can happen to a trainer who fails to take culture into account comes from a colleague who was new to an organisation. He had been used to running management skills programmes for various organisations but was now trying to run a tailored programme for his new employer.

On one programme a course member said that a particular problem for his office team was that they had far too much work to do. The trainer suggested that overtime was one possible solution.

It was unfortunate that the trainer had not done more research before making that suggestion because working overtime was something which most of the staff in this organisation did not agree with. It was an 'issue' for this organisation – contrary to most of the staff's norms and values, except in extraordinary circumstances. The trainer lost a lot of credibility because the course members felt he did not understand the culture; that he did not understand 'the ways things are done around here'.

Another example is the way in which many trainers have tried to help their organisations to respond to the effects of a more rapidly changing marketplace coupled with changes to the demographic composition of the work force. Some trainers have tried to change the traditional ways of management thinking. The 'old' solutions no longer fit the 'new' problems.

To meet this need many trainers have moved away from traditional 'knowledge and skills' courses and brought out a new range of courses which worked with learners' attitudes and behaviours. However, many trainers have discovered that these training programmes are met with suspicion, and even hostility. In many cases the problem has been that the old culture within the organisation remains very strong. The old culture includes many assumptions about what to expect from a training course and a trainer's role. Suddenly these assumptions and values are being threatened and challenged. In some cases the training has 'worked' but in many cases people have seen the situation as threatening and responded by being negative, defensive, withdrawn or hostile. The trainers have not taken culture into account.

To improve your awareness of culture and the implications for training, read through the Recognising Culture Checklist and then work through the next five activities. These will show you how others see the culture of your organisation, introduce some common assumptions and values and point out where the main areas of difference occur.

Recognising culture checklist

How can you recognise culture? Often we are aware of culture on a subliminal as well as conscious level. The following checklist is by no means exhaustive but it will give you a guide as to what to look for.

1) Physical signs

a) The way people dress: uniforms, rules about whether jackets can be removed or sleeves rolled up, whether casual clothes or formal clothing such as suits may be worn, colours, corporate styles and colours.
b) Office layouts: open plan, private offices, more senior people seated where they can observe and control more easily or in preferred places (next to a window or a radiator for example), amount of space between desks, positioning of desks to ease discussion or minimise it, whether the quality of furnishings is related to seniority or job function.
c) Noise level and music.
d) Building design: purpose built, makeshift, functional, pleasing to the eye, taking human needs as well as business needs into account.

2) Way of life at work

a) Work ethics.
b) Management and leadership styles.
c) How ideas are expressed and treated.
d) Styles and methods of communication.
e) How emotions are expressed and dealt with.
f) Degree and type of rules, procedures, freedom.
g) Methods of evaluating performance, reward, promotion.
h) How external pressures and requirements are dealt with – for example, legislative requirements, customer demands, competitors.
i) Pace of working life, hours worked, breaks and time off.
j) Language, acronyms, jargon.

Reproduced from *Dealing with Difference*
by Teresa Williams and Adrian Green, Gower, Aldershot, 1994.

3) Published aspects

a) Company logo.
b) Corporate plan or general business plan.
c) Mission and vision statements.
d) Quality statements or customer charter.
e) Advertising literature for products.
f) Advertising literature for new recruits.
g) Training and development plans, statements, schemes, course specifications.
f) Annual report and accounts.
g) Minutes of meetings, for example AGM, EGM, shareholders' meetings, board meetings, external liaison meetings.
h) Appraisal and job evaluation procedures.

4) Underlying assumptions

Less tangible, and often unspoken, aspects (unless an individual does not conform) are underlying assumptions, such as:

a) What is regarded as good or acceptable practice.
b) When it is acceptable not to follow the modus operandi.
c) How much individualism is acceptable.
d) To what extent people are expected to follow the rules even on occasions when the rules don't seem to make sense.

Reproduced from *Dealing with Difference*
by Teresa Williams and Adrian Green, Gower, Aldershot, 1994.

Activity 1	For trainers

Perceptions

Purpose

This first activity is designed to increase your awareness of how other people perceive the culture of an organisation for which you have a training responsibility. It is specifically designed to:

- focus on the differences and similarities in perceptions at different levels of the hierarchy

and

- find out if there is any relationship between the length of time individuals have worked for the organisation and their perception of the organisation's culture.

Method

- Familiarise yourself with the Recognising Culture checklist (pages 18–19). You may wish to photocopy the pages and have it ready to help you.
- Choose at least four people to interview informally:
  - Someone who has recently joined the organisation at a more junior level.
  - Someone who has recently joined the organisation at a more senior level.
  - Someone long-serving and junior.
  - Someone long-serving and senior.

- Spend ten to fifteen minutes asking each of the people you have chosen how they perceive the culture of the organisation. If they do not know how to start describing the culture use the checklist as a prompt.

Note: It is best to wait to see which aspects of the culture they focus on, the words they use to describe it, and what aspects they do not mention. Try not to lead them by giving your perceptions. Most people have a view on the organisation's culture even though they may not be conscious of exactly what they mean by culture.

Debrief

- Look at the four different responses and check for similarities and differences.
- How did the responses compare with your expectations? Are there any surprises?
- What common perceived strengths or assets are there about the organisation's culture?
- What common perceived weaknesses or liabilities are there about the organisation's culture?

Conclusion

Becoming more aware of how the organisation's culture is perceived is the first step towards taking it into account from a training point of view. The view that trainers have of an organisation is often quite different from that of the ordinary workers because trainers may be:

- In closer touch with senior management.
- More likely to understand the corporate plan (where there is one).
- Aware of issues at a more strategic level.
- A little more removed from the main work of the organisation because they are part of a separate training or human resourcing department, or are external to the organisation.

If the responses you received were in line with what you expected, ask yourself what it is that helps you to keep so well in touch. Try to maintain that communication.

If the responses contained some surprises then consider what action you can take to increase your awareness of:

- The organisation's culture.
- How the culture is perceived in different areas.
- How the culture is perceived at different levels and by people with different lengths of service.

For trainers

The culture in which you operate

Purpose

This activity is designed to help you to:
- Focus on the culture of your own section or department

and
- Recognise how that culture differs from the rest of the organisation.

Method

- Using the Recognising Culture Checklist (pages 18–19) to help you, describe the culture of your own section or department. Use the four headings:
  - Physical signs.
  - Working way of life.
  - Published aspects.
  - Underlying assumptions.
- Analyse the culture of your section to see how it differs from the rest of the organisation. You can use the information you gathered for Activity 1 to help you.

Debrief

Some issues you can explore are:

- How is your section's culture regarded by people in other parts of the organisation? For example, is it seen as 'not being in the real world' or as 'a role model to work towards' or as 'practising what they preach'?
- Are people in your section so closely entrenched in their culture that they are ineffective when it comes to helping the organisation to change (when appropriate)?

Conclusion

Consider how well you, and the people in your section, are equipped to help others to learn and develop. How well equipped are you to help others to change in some way? If the culture in which you work is itself resistant to change what effect will that have on the people you are trying to help?

Consider what you can do to encourage the culture of your section to be one which can help the organisation and the people within it to develop. At the same time how can you encourage the culture of your section not to be so different that you are seen as being unrealistic, or 'living in another world'?

For trainers

Your section's culture as seen by its members

Purpose

This activity is particularly valuable if you are a member of an in-house training section or part of a training team which works closely together on learning events. It encourages you to explore the differences in perceptions which members have about the culture of your section.

Method

- Explain to each member that you are trying to understand the culture of your section and the differences in how it is seen. This is so that you can work more effectively together.
- Ask each one to explain their perception of the section's culture. They can do it anonymously in writing or, preferably, through face to face discussion with you on an individual or group basis. To give a structure to your analysis you can use the four headings:
    - Physical signs.
    - Working way of life.
    - Published aspects.
    - Underlying assumptions.

Debrief

Compare the similarities and differences of each person's perceptions of the section's culture. Compare your perceptions with theirs.

Why do you think these similarities and differences exist?

Conclusion

Some examples of conclusions that other training sections have come to are:

- Some members viewed the autocratic management style as helpful and as an example of strong leadership, whereas others thought it was stifling to creativity and initiative.
- One section had a strong published statement of its values and beliefs in relation to training. Many members of the section did not really believe in what was stated although they pretended to. This led to limited progress through lack of commitment.
- Someone who had recently joined a training department with a very strong culture found it difficult to apply their own ideas, even though these were very appropriate to issues in hand. Their ideas were seen as a threat to the established ways of doing things rather than as ideas for making improvements.

For trainers

Assumptions we make

Purpose

This activity will help you to start to identify your own cultural assumptions and mindsets about learners in general, or about specific groups of learners.

Method

Assumptions are ideas you take for granted and conclusions you reach without real proof. You can help pinpoint some of the assumptions you make by either thinking about a learning event which is taking place soon, or about one which has recently finished.

Some classic examples of assumptions which you hear trainers make are that 'they always learn better through participation' or 'this one's nearing retirement and won't want to be bothered with all these changes'.

Using Diagram 3 to help, write down ten assumptions which you tend to make about learners.

Debrief

Consider the implications of your assumptions:

- How would you help a learner who does not fit the stereotype you expect?
- How would you help a learner who fits your expectations?
- What can you do to accommodate different learners?
- What can you do to move from assumptions to evidence?

Conclusion

Identifying and working on your own assumptions will help you to empathise with the learners with whom you are in contact. You will

	Assumption		Implications
1			
2			
3			
4			
5			
6			
7			
8			
9			
10			

One positive action I'm going to take as a result of this activity is …

28 | **Diagram 3.** Assumptions we make

also be in a better position to recognise and deal with the assumptions they are making about the learning process.

It is worthwhile checking with other trainers in your organisation to see whether or not their assumptions are the same or different to yours. If the same assumptions are being made by all the trainers are you missing an opportunity, are you blind to certain possibilities? Are different trainers trying to pull the organisation in different ways because of different assumptions and hence counteracting or negating each other's efforts?

For trainers

Belongingness

Purpose

This activity is designed to help you to raise your awareness of the cultural groups with which you are associated, and the implications for you as a trainer.

It looks first at the cultural groups to which you belong. These could be, for example, a department, trade union, sports group, functional group, family or social group, or a geographically based group (such as a branch away from the parent organisation).

The next stage is to discover how the values and beliefs of each of the groups influence the way in which you work.

Example 1: 'There is an "us and them" conflict between this site and the one the other side of town which leads to considerable intolerance and competitiveness on both sides. We're all caught up in it even though it's so unhealthy for our company.'

Example 2: 'There is a strong tradition of teamwork in this section. It is not supported by the rest of the organisation where merit is rewarded on a solely individual basis.'

Example 3: 'I'm in a conflict because my work group expects confidentiality to be respected but my colleagues in other departments expect me to tell stories about what happens with the people I interact with.'

Method

Spend a few minutes considering each of the items given below.

- Of which cultural groups are you a member? (At work and during your non-working hours.)
- How do the values and beliefs of each of the groups influence the way in which you work?

Debrief

Debrief and consolidate by completing the following: (You may need to write different answers relating to the different cultural groups of which you are a member.)

In terms of my work as a trainer:

- The potential strengths of the values and beliefs of the cultural groups to which I belong are ...
- The potential drawbacks of the values and beliefs are ...

Conclusion

Many trainers find that particular values and beliefs strongly influence the way in which they work. For example, a colleague ranks family needs very highly and will arrange wherever possible for either a programme to finish by 5.00 p.m., or for someone else to take over.

Another colleague will not run a programme unless confidentiality is guaranteed. This can cause a serious difference of opinion when a client organisation does not share a belief in the need for confidentiality.

It is important to be aware of the values and beliefs of the cultural groups to which you belong because these will influence the way in which you train. You need to recognise when your values and beliefs differ from those with whom you are involved, such as the senior management of an organisation or learners.

Summary

Our working definition of culture is:

'meanings, beliefs, understandings, values and assumptions subscribed to by a group of people'.

You can improve your awareness of culture and its implications by learning to:

- Recognise culture in terms of physical signs, way of life, published aspects, underlying assumptions, and so on.
- See how people with different levels of seniority and length of service perceive the culture of their organisation.
- Identify similarities and differences in the way in which a culture is perceived.
- Recognise how the training culture is perceived and why.
- Explore the assumptions, values and beliefs you hold as a trainer.

3 | The trainer's role

It is worth spending some time exploring your own role as a trainer and its cultural implications. Let's look first at some of the reasons why you may have asked, or been asked, to be involved with a particular piece of training and development.

Why you?

- **Expertise.**

It may be that you have particular expertise for which you are well respected. This expertise may be related to your in-depth knowledge of a particular organisation. It may be because of your specialist expertise in a particular discipline, such as training staff to sell Contract X. Or your expertise may be of a more general nature such as training design for management development and interpersonal skills.

- **Availability.**

You may be the person who is available, or who has some spare capacity at the time when the training work is needed.

- **Independent advice.**

You may be seen as being able to stand back and provide an independent and unbiased service. You may be a member of a training or human resourcing department who can act confidentially and without reporting to other departments. You may be able to take a neutral stand when different departments are in conflict.

- **Status.**

An external trainer may be brought in for reasons of status and 'respectability'. Management can say that it has 'brought in an expert'. This can be important in attaching credibility to an idea which has been proposed internally but which has met with little response. If you are an employee you may be chosen because your job title or level within the organisation affords you some special status.

- **Blame.**

The trainer in 'the ivory tower' or who is external can be made an easy target if things do not work out. Managers within the organisation can disown responsibility all too easily if there is a problem.

- **Confidentiality.**

Trainers can often provide an environment in which learners can freely discuss issues without being concerned with how they will be judged, whether their career will be affected, how senior management will view them or what their managers will think of them.

Where do you fit in?

Often you may be asked to be involved with a learning event for more than one of the reasons given above but whatever they are, stop for a moment to consider the implications of culture for the learning and development process.

For example, if you suspect that you have been chosen so that senior management can try to disclaim responsibility if there is a problem, then explore the assumptions, values and beliefs underlying the process before you become too immersed. It can be more productive to spend time on managing those differences than in completing very extensive course design.

If you have been selected because you are seen to be the expert then consider:

- What assumptions, values and beliefs are there surrounding that premise?
- What are the implications both for the way in which your training will be initially received and then valued in the longer term?
- To what extent will you be able to match up to expectations of you as an expert – do you share them?
- If you have been selected because the culture demands that an expert acts in a particular way, but you act in another way, will it undermine the effectiveness of the learning process?

Assess some of the different learning events with which you have been involved in the following way:

- Why were you selected to design or run that learning event?

What was your role?

- What were the assumptions, values and beliefs of those who appointed you?
- Were there any differences in values from the ones you held at the time?
- How did any cultural similarities or differences affect the effectiveness of the learning process?

You may not be able to answer the questions fully for learning events in the past. However, these are questions which will help you with learning events in the future.

Summary

Why is it *you* who carries out a particular training function?

How does that relate to the culture in which you operate?

What are the implications for the learning and development process?

You may have been asked to be involved with a learning event because of your:

- Expertise.
- Availability.
- Ability to give independent advice.
- Status or perceived status.
- Position as an easy target to blame if things go wrong.
- Ability to provide confidentiality.

Explore the assumptions, values and beliefs underlying the reason why you are involved with any particular learning event.

37

Part II — Learners from different cultural groups

Introduction to Part II

So far, we have established our working definition of culture and have discussed how to recognise culture. We have also explored some of the cultural biases we, as trainers, will be influenced by. Now let's move on and examine some cultural groups and how you can make use of this knowledge to help the learning and development process.

You can become aware of the implications of culture on the learning and development process by exploring different cultural groups. Many studies have been conducted on the culture of different countries, religious groups, occupational groups and so on. In this section we explore two areas:

- Organisational culture and its implications for the learning and development process

and

- National differences in values and behaviour. (This section explains the dimensions of culture identified by Geert Hofstede.)

In both areas theory and practice are interwoven so that you can apply the concepts to your work as a trainer.

4 | Organisational culture

Why should we explore organisational culture? What is its relationship to the learning and development process? Arthur Young (1986) says: 'As a trainer it is important for you to know the official company culture (stated values) and to compare it with reality.' There may well be one stated and dominant culture but you are also likely to find a number of sub-cultures in different departments, branches or levels of hierarchy.

Let's examine:
- What organisational culture is
- How you can observe it

and then
- How that might influence the design and delivery of learning and development events.

What is organisational culture?

Michael Armstrong (1989) defines corporate culture in this way. 'Corporate culture is the pattern of shared attitudes, beliefs, assumptions and expectations which shape the way people act and interact in an organisation and underpin the way things get done.'

The culture of any organisation is based on norms and core values. Norms are those unwritten rules about how to behave. Norms sometimes contravene the written rules. Core values are based on what is seen as right and wrong.

Every group generates its own norms. Consider a visit to a hotel you have never visited before. How does your behaviour differ from a visit to a hotel with which you are familiar? Why should there *be* a difference? The answer for many people is that they are a little reserved when they arrive at an unfamiliar hotel. They do not know what the form is. They may be asking themselves 'Do I need to order a newspaper every day or does the order on the first day get repeated for the rest of my stay? Do I need a key if I stay out late or is there a night porter? Is it acceptable to ask for photocopying after 5.00 p.m. even though they say they offer a 24-hour office service?'

Each hotel will have its own norms. Hotels in the same chain may well have some norms in common, and these may well be documented, but each hotel will also develop a unique set of unwritten rules. These norms are rarely written in the hotel brochure and to establish them you have to ask, observe or find out by trial and error. Sometimes you might find out about them by asking a colleague who has stayed there before.

There are norms or unwritten rules about almost every aspect of life at work. There are norms that relate to how interviews should be handled, how circulars should be written and distributed, how meetings and discussions should take place, how the managers and teams work together.

Core values are based on what is seen as good and bad. Values and norms need to support each other for culture to be strong and harmonious.

The core values may be set by senior management but they may or may not be subscribed to by others in the organisation. For example, senior management may assert that customer care is of paramount importance – that the customer is always right and should be treated with respect at all times. Yet you may find there are large areas of your organisation where people, at all levels, treat the customer as just another order number.

Changing values

Organisational culture changes over time. People's ideas of what is good and bad change (their values change), and so they no longer like or agree with the norms (the rules which support what is good or bad). A classic and easy to recognise example is smoking at work. Most people in the UK now consider smoking to be bad (a value judgement) and this has lead to a change in the rules and expectations about where and when people should and should not smoke (a norm). Education and training have effected this change by, for example:

- Helping to alter people's views of what is good and bad by passing on medical findings.
- Informing people about the new rules, and helping them to overcome any difficulties in conforming to them.

44 Another example of differences in norms comes from a colleague work-

ing on a secondment in India. She noticed soon after arriving that there was a substantial difference in the standard of course handouts produced in her UK office and those in India. She felt the ones produced in India were very poorly presented, but nobody else seemed to be concerned and nobody responded to her suggestion that handouts should be improved.

After some time she asked one of the more senior staff, whom she had come to know well, if she was trying to impose her own values inappropriately. She was not sure her cultural beliefs were acceptable or understood; perhaps the Indian office had very different beliefs and values. On some issues their norms seemed to be quite different.

After some discussion she found that the people in the Indian office did prefer their UK head office standards on course handouts but did not know how to achieve them. (My colleague had thought it sufficient to point out the differences and to state what she would like to see.) She wished she had explored the differences in values and beliefs earlier because now she knew how to set about changing the norms (the unwritten rules) in relation to the issue of high quality course handouts.

Finding out about an organisation's culture

You can start by examining various public statements produced by the organisation: the mission statement, vision statement, corporate philosophy as espoused, the annual report and accounts, customer care or quality statements and the corporate plan. Activity 6 on pages 47–8 will help you to explore these public aspects of an organisation's culture.

Significance of your findings

By learning about corporate or organisational culture you can tune into the assumptions, values and beliefs which the organisation espouses and which the senior management may adhere to. Later in your analysis you can find out whether a learner on your event belongs to a section which shares the same cultural values or whether those values are different from the main organisation's culture.

You can then explore the material and style of the learning event to see if it conforms to the learner's culture. If it is different you can find out whether it is likely to affect the transfer of learning on return to work.

Think back to a learning event where members came from different parts of your organisation. The event may well have been designed to take account of overall organisational requirements. However, there may have been some learners who immediately subscribed to the learn-

45

ing and others who found it much more difficult to relate the learning to their environment. Sometimes a learning event may conform to corporate culture but not sectional culture.

Not taking account of different cultures was one of the difficulties which many of the total quality management, (TQM) implementors of the 1980s faced. The same training was delivered in the same way across the whole organisation which resulted in some areas finding it easy to fit TQM into their working environment and others finding it much more difficult. Progress and effectiveness of the TQM programme were therefore variable.

If the culture of the learning event is different from both the sectional and corporate cultures are there other support structures in place to help the transfer of learning? Culture is deep-seated and often subconscious and there needs to be a good reason for attempting to change it.

For trainers

Published organisational culture

Purpose

You may gain some insight into an organisation's culture from aspects which are consciously published, either orally or in writing.

The purpose of this activity is to help you gather a better picture of the published aspects of the organisation's culture so that you may explore the idea of whether the actual culture is supported by – or contradictory to – the published culture. Does the training and development you are involved with support or contradict the published cultural image?

Examples of oral publishing of culture are presentations of annual reports to employees or shareholders, briefing groups and video recordings. Written examples include quality care statements, report and accounts, mission and vision statements, and advertising literature.

Method

- Complete the Published Organisational Culture Activity on pages 49–50 as fully as possible. It may be that you do not usually have access to certain information. You may have to be assertive or creative in obtaining it.
- To gain a full picture talk to people at different levels; look through advertising literature for jobs or products; study back copies of the in-house journal or briefing sheets; look at posters in the reception area on quality or corporate approach.

Debrief

- Summarise the culture in three or four sentences based on the information which you now have.
- From what you know about the culture already (for example from the information gained in the previous activities given in this book) are the real culture and the published culture one and the same?

- If there are differences:
  - What are they?
  - Why do you think this is so?
- If there are similarities what has helped to achieve them?

Conclusions

Quite often senior management publishes and operates culture at senior levels which is not actively supported at lower levels. This is often due to poor communication.

If you believe in the culture as published, or in the culture which senior management promotes, does the training and development you are involved with help or hinder? Is it consistent with or contrary to the values and beliefs held by senior management?

Published organisational culture

Make some notes on your organisation's culture under the following headings:

The organisation's mission and vision statements

Corporate philosophy as given in the annual report and accounts

Customer care or quality statements

Reproduced from *Dealing with Difference*
by Teresa Williams and Adrian Green, Gower, Aldershot, 1994.

Core values set by senior management

Any other published statements about the organisation's values and beliefs

50

For trainers

Comparing organisational cultures

Purpose

By collecting examples of published aspects of organisational culture in different organisations you can compare and contrast the different messages. You can see how weakly or strongly they are portrayed. It will help you to recognise different espoused organisational cultures. You can then compare your findings with the espoused organisational culture of the organisation for which you work.

Method

- Collect some examples of different mission and vision statements, sets of core values and organisation philosophies. Try to collect information from at least three or four different organisations. You can find such information in many places, including:
  - Posters in company reception areas.
  - Quality statements on customer literature.
  - Annual reports and accounts.
  - Christmas messages.
  - Product literature.
  - Recruitment literature.
  - In-house journal or newsletter.
  - Open-day advertising literature.
  - Information given to schools visits / projects.
  - Induction literature.
  - Advertisements.

Debrief

- How does the information vary for the different organisations?
- What does that tell you about their different cultures – or
   at least about the cultures and images they are trying to portray, even if they are not true in reality?
- From what you know so far about these organisations what do

you suspect or deduce about their attitudes towards learning and development?

● If you wanted to know more about the implications of organisational culture on the learning and development process within these organisations what aspects would you follow up in more detail?

Conclusion

If you work mainly with one organisation it is all too easy to become so engrossed in its culture that you cannot see that there are alternative approaches. By examining other organisational cultures and images you may gain some new ideas on helping your own organisation with its learning and development process.

In one organisation the key trainer found it useful to study different ways of putting across senior management norms and values. The senior managers had not been communicating their norms and values effectively to the rest of the organisation. By becoming more aware of different approaches she was able to help senior management personnel develop their communication skills in order to transmit those norms and values effectively.

Activity 8 | For trainers

Sectional culture

Purpose

The purpose of this activity is to help you study the culture of a particular section of an organisation with the aim of analysing the implications of that culture on the learning and development process. This will give you more specific information than you obtain by studying the culture of an organisation as a whole.

The subculture which you have chosen to study may be representative of the main organisation's culture or it may be quite different, as often happens in cases of geographically remote branches, physically separated buildings or different functional areas.

Method

- Choose a section of the organisation which you would like to study. It may be easier to choose one with which you normally have contact in the course of your work, rather than seem to be suddenly taking an unnatural interest in an unfamiliar section. It would also be useful if it is a section for which you have to organise or deliver some training so that the activity has a practical purpose.
- First note down the visual aspects of the section's culture. For example, look at office layout, clothing, seating positions for meetings, age groups (refer to Recognising Culture Checklist on pages 18–19).
- Then look at written aspects. Look at the type of posters and written notices on the walls, the style and content of letters, memos, reports.
- See what you can find out about underlying assumptions and values by studying management style, the way in which difficult situations are handled, the general atmosphere and conversational style, codes of conduct and ethics, operational style.

Debrief

- What are the implications for technical training in this section?
- What are the implications for training in managerial and inter-personal skills?
- To what extent does the culture concentrate on supporting the task in hand or supporting the people in the section?
- If a new method, technique or technology had to be implemented in this section in which ways do you think the culture would help and hinder?

Conclusion

One example of how you may conclude your findings is shown through the following case. A section of an organisation had a very close, protective, paternalistic culture, where nobody wanted to change the established ways of doing things and where there were many set procedures for handling the various situations which had to be dealt with. Setting up and implementing a new administrative system for a new contract was proving to be more difficult than expected.

However, the process was eventually helped significantly by training people to set up their *own* new procedures – this helped them feel less threatened and less at risk. Training based on the technical aspects of the new system alone was not enough. Other needs had to be addressed, based on their protective, paternalistic culture.

Once you understand the existing culture there are many approaches you can take to help a section with training and development. You can train in a way that is supportive of the existing culture, or train in a way that challenges or attempts to change the existing culture. In either case it can be very helpful to:

- Consciously recognise the culture of the section at that moment.
- Recognise the strengths and weaknesses in relation to the learning and development process.
- Decide where it would be helpful for the culture to remain the same and where a change would be more beneficial.

How close are you?

Let's explore the effect which your closeness to the organisation's prevailing culture may have on the learning and development process. There are advantages and disadvantages both to being very close to the culture of the organisation which you are trying to help and to not subscribing to the same assumptions, values and beliefs. Let's examine first the implications of the trainer and organisation subscribing to the same culture.

Sharing the same culture

If the values and beliefs you hold are very close to those of the organisation are you really in the best position to provide the help people need?

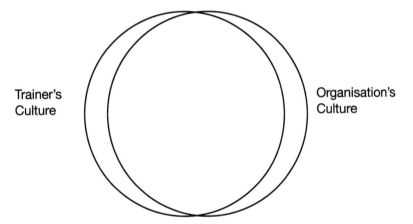

Trainer's Culture

Organisation's Culture

Diagram 4. Sharing the same culture

If you are very close to the organisation's culture and if you subscribe to many of the same assumptions, values and beliefs you will enjoy the following advantages. You will be more easily able to:

- Strengthen and nurture the existing culture and way of doing things.
- Help the organisation to grow within existing values and beliefs.
- Maintain the status quo.
- Recognise options that will be readily acceptable, non-threatening and consistent with the existing culture.
- Talk the same language. People may feel that they are being understood.

However, there are also disadvantages to being very close to the organisation's current culture and subscribing to many of the same assumptions, values and beliefs. These can include:

- Being too entrenched in the existing culture and therefore not strong enough to facilitate change where needed.
- Not recognising that other options have advantages for the organisation.
- Feeling uncomfortable with other approaches and so not communicating them in a positive and convincing way – body language speaking more loudly than words.
- Not being seen as representative of the new culture towards which the organisation is trying to move (that is, not being seen to be an expert in or currently practising what is being espoused).

Subscribing to different cultures

It may be that you are very distant in terms of culture from the organisation you are trying to help. This means that you subscribe to quite different assumptions, values and beliefs.

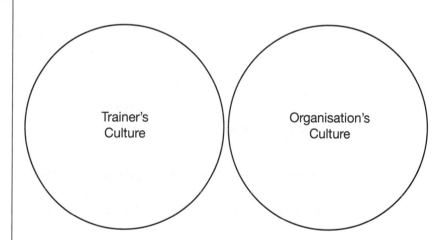

Diagram 5.   Subscribing to different cultures

The potential advantages of subscribing to a different culture include:

- Not being intimidated by the organisation's values and beliefs as they are not consistent with your own.
- Being 'untainted' and fresh and ready to put forward new ideas and ways of doing things.

- Being a living demonstration of the different culture, providing a role model.

Potential disadvantages include:

- Not speaking enough of the same language to gain the respect and understanding you need to initiate change.
- Not being able to build bridges between the existing and the desired culture.
- An inability to show empathy.
- Inability of the client to recognise that you have something of value to offer because your assumptions seem so different.

In addition to these two extreme positions there are of course many halfway stages. Only in exceptional circumstances are a trainer and an organisation so completely similar or distant.

Here are some questions which you might like to debate at this point:

- How close or distant are you in relation to the organisation(s) or individual(s) you are trying to help?
- Are you too entrenched in the culture or are you too distant? Why do you believe this to be the case?
- What positive steps can you take to move to a more appropriate position? (If you feel you are in an appropriate position, what can you do to maintain it?)

Summary

Organisational culture is based on 'the way in which things get done around here'.

There are norms which are (usually) unwritten rules about how to behave.

There are values which are based on what is seen as good or bad.

When the values (what is good and bad) are supported by the norms (unwritten rules) then the culture is strong and harmonious. However, norms and values change over time.

Study your organisation's published culture and compare it with reality.

Compare your organisation's culture with other organisational cultures.

Study the differences in any organisation's culture by exploring and comparing the culture of individual sections.

Assess to what extent you subscribe to the organisation's assumptions, values and beliefs. Does that help or hinder what you are trying (or are required) to achieve?

There are times when subscribing to the organisation's culture is appropriate and helpful to the learning and development process. There are other times when there can be distinct advantages to the learning and development process if you are of a more distant culture or if you subscribe to a quite different culture.

5 | National differences

The purpose of this book is to help you to be more effective as a trainer by recognising and managing the implications of culture for the learning and development process.

This section on national culture aims to introduce you to some work that has been done at a country or national level. But it does not provide the kind of stereotypical approach that says Americans have this type of culture, French this type, and so on. The purpose is to provide tools and a model that you can apply to situations which you personally face.

So long as you do not stereotype the particular learners in your group it is useful to examine culture on a broader level. In any nation there will be a wide range of mini-cultures, some of which may be very different from the national culture as a whole.

National culture can have a strong influence on many people – a much stronger influence in some nations than others. One aspect of national culture is that via education, the media, and so on, status or prestige is given to particular achievements. For example, in America some of the culture groupings respect and admire individualism, so you will find many developing professionals who aspire to being pioneers in their chosen fields and to individual achievements. Another example of the influence of national culture is where nationals are expected to buy goods produced in their own country rather than imported goods.

Hofstede's work

Some learners can experience distress and withdrawal from the learning process if the values and norms being discussed during training conflict with those of their national culture, especially when they wholeheartedly subscribe to a very strong national culture.

There are many ways of analysing and categorising national culture. Geert Hofstede (1984, 1991) is a Dutch professor who has conducted extensive research into national differences in over 50 countries. He identified four main dimensions in which national cultures can be analysed and rated. Hofstede's more recent work in this area has identified additional issues but in this book we will explore the four main dimensions which he identified originally. They provide a widely recognised framework for discussing and analysing cultural differences.

Hofstede's research is relevant to those working for an organisation which has branches in different countries, to those who buy or sell in foreign countries, to people developing joint ventures within two or more countries, and to those who employ people of different nationalities. It is useful to all those involved with multinational and multicultural organisations. It is also useful for people working in smaller organisations because in any organisation there are different subcultures and Hofstede's work gives us a way of describing them.

In all these cases then, we can look at the implications of Hofstede's dimensions of culture for the learning and development process.

As a definition of culture Hofstede uses 'the collective programming of the mind which distinguishes the members of one human group from another'. He does not see this as a complete definition of culture but as one which covers the areas he has been able to measure through his research.

Although Hofstede's work examines the similarities and differences in culture patterns of over 50 different countries, it is important from a trainer's point of view not to make stereotypical assumptions about everyone from a particular country because of the traits or patterns which may emerge from studying the people as a whole. There will always be individual differences.

Before we can apply Hofstede's work to learning and development situations we need to examine his four dimensions and what he meant by them. The four dimensions are:

- Power distance.
- Uncertainty avoidance.
- Individualism/ collectivism.
- Masculinity/ femininity.

Power distance

The power-distance dimension relates to the inequality which exists in life. There is inequality in many areas of life – differences in money, status, power, ownership of property and rights. It exists within work organisations, in social organisations, in clans, tribes and nations. Inequality has been the subject of discussion and analysis for centuries and different groups have found many different solutions.

In any business organisation there are differences in the way power, wealth, status and rewards are distributed. The basis for determining these inequalities are often set out in hierarchy charts, contracts, procedures and plans. Power distance in an organisation relates to the extent to which subordinates feel they can disagree with their manager, can influence decisions made by their manager and can participate in the decision making process.

In Hofstede's research, in high power-distance countries (that is, where there is a large distance or inequality between bosses and subordinates), subordinates are afraid of, or prefer not to get involved in, the decision making process. Subordinates expect their boss to lead, make decisions and to direct without involving them. Where there is a high power-distance culture we are more likely to see a preference for a directive and autocratic style of management. We are more likely to see characteristics such as dependency by subordinates on more senior levels, lower levels blamed for mistakes and problems and little trust. Those in a position of power are likely to try to appear as powerful as possible. Bosses and subordinates are more likely to regard each other as 'different species'.

Where there is a low power-distance culture we are more likely to see characteristics such as more interdependence between boss and subordinate, a preference for more equal rights, a greater willingness to trust each other and not to see each other as a threat. People in a position of power will try to appear less powerful than they really are.

Implications for trainers

There are many implications which spring to mind:

- **How the trainer is perceived.**
  In a high power-distance culture the trainer may be perceived as being in a similar category to the boss. Hence there may be expectations that the trainer will lead, direct, tell them the right way to do things and take total responsibility for the learning process.
- **Mismatch between cultures.**
  If the trainer is of a low power-distance culture and the learners are of a high power-distance culture there are likely to be frustrations on both sides. The trainer may feel that the learners want to be led too much, are not contributing, are unresponsive and uncooperative. The learners may feel that the trainer is not doing a proper job, is avoiding the issue, is not structured or prepared.

- **Self managed learning.**

For self managed learning to be effective it is necessary for the learner to take responsibility, for the learner to direct the learning process, for the boss to be a mentor and help where needed or when asked to. In other words these are features of a low power-distance culture.

You can probably now recognise that some organisations have tried to implement some form of self managed learning in a strong high power-distance culture. You can probably also recognise some of the reasons why it may not have proved a very effective learning and development process.

- **The return to work.**

Many traditional training methods require that learners be debriefed and coached by their managers on return to work. But we all know many cases of managers who seem unwilling to make this happen.

If a manager subscribes to a high power-distance culture and a learner comes back with new ideas and new methods the manager may see it as a threat. Then the manager either ignores the new ideas to protect the existing status quo, or acts in a directive way saying 'forget all those new ideas on the course – they don't work. In this section we do it like this.'

If the learner prefers to operate in a low power-distance culture such an attitude will lead to frustration, intolerance, withdrawal, even a decision to leave the organisation. Some learners with courage will challenge the system, of course, but often they will be seen as disruptive elements. A few will gradually chip away at old patterns and bring in new ideas.

Other learners, who prefer to subscribe to the high power-distance culture, will quietly accept that the ideas they discussed on the training course may work elsewhere but are not appropriate for their section. The trainers will be blamed for not living in the real world.

Many of the people from the high power-distance culture probably do not know why they were sent on the course in the first place. However, their attendance means that their appraisal or training record form can be updated and filled in for that year.

Uncertainty avoidance

Hofstede's uncertainty avoidance dimension examines the extent to which we try to avoid uncertainty; the extent of an individual's ability to cope with different levels of uncertainty. Some cultural groupings seem considerably more at ease coping with uncertainty than others.

Different cultures have developed different ways of coping with uncertainty, such as the use of laws, procedures, religion, research, statistical tools, strategic planning, rituals and rules.

In any given situation some individuals will have a greater need to deal with the uncertainty which they perceive. The tolerance level of a group of people to deal with perceived uncertainty or to avoid that uncertainty is called Hofstede's Uncertainty Avoidance Index.

Someone with a higher level of tolerance for uncertainty (or low uncertainty avoidance in Hofstede's terms) may do such things as:

- Break the rules if they feel the situation warrants it.
- Refuse to follow a procedure if they feel it is inappropriate in a particular case.
- Disagree with an established way of handling a situation if they feel it is no longer appropriate.
- Be more prepared to work in new situations or in new roles, or to break new ground in a field.
- Experiment freely and often.
- Take more risks, be less resistant to change.
- Fight for general guidelines within which they can use their own initiative rather than be restricted by tight rules and procedures.

They are also more like to cope better with ambiguous and poorly defined situations.

Someone with a lower level of tolerance for uncertainty (high uncertainty avoidance in Hofstede's terms) is likely to prefer:

- Rules and procedures for dealing with as many situations as possible.
- Established and approved guidelines for handling difficult situations.
- To avoid situations which are new and untested, such as a new job, a new role, working for a different organisation, moving house.
- Group decision making rather than making decisions themselves.
- Using tried and tested methods.
- Taking fewer risks.

They tend to be more afraid of failure and to cope less well with ambiguous situations.

Implications for trainers

- How much uncertainty can you cope with as a trainer? What is the accepted norm for the group to which you belong? How set or how flexible do you need a learning event to be?

  Answers to these questions will have an impact on what you can comfortably provide for learners. Some trainers like to be more unstructured and flexible about the timetable but this may be difficult for learners with a low level of tolerance for uncertainty.

- Is there a difference between the uncertainty level that you can cope with and the norm for the other trainers with whom you work?

  The answer has important implications in many areas, such as how detailed trainer notes need to be, how detailed the liaison between co-trainers needs to be and how much the learning event can be changed while it is in progress to respond to learners' needs.

- If you are running an activity or practical exercise, learners with a low tolerance for uncertainty may prefer detailed instructions, guidelines and examples to follow. They may be looking for a 'right' answer from the trainer at the end.

- Learners with a low tolerance for uncertainty may find role playing more threatening for several reasons: it requires them to experiment, to take risks; there may not be a 'right' procedure to follow; it may be a previously untested and untried situation; they may be afraid of failure.

- Learners with a higher tolerance for uncertainty may request (and be disappointed if not provided with) opportunities to experiment, discuss and use walk-throughs relating to real situations that they face.

- When it comes to transferring the learning back to work those with a higher tolerance for uncertainty may be more prepared to experiment. Those with a lower tolerance can be helped by using practise walk-throughs, detailed action plans, forward planning of the first steps of implementation, coaching and support from their manager, and a colleague's help in implementing ideas.

Individualism/collectivism

Individualism/collectivism is the third dimension which Hofstede identified in his research. It concerns the extent to which people think and act as individuals, based on their own self-determination, as opposed to conforming or adhering to the ways of a group of people (the collective view of an organisation or a family, for example). A number of Western cultures are regarded as being more individualistic than many Eastern societies. Of course there are many variations.

In an individualistic culture great store is set in following your own convictions, taking your own needs into account as a priority, 'doing your own thing', being independent of others. In a collectivist culture the success and effectiveness of the group as a whole is regarded as being more important than any one individual's needs. This may involve individual members making personal sacrifices for the good of the group as a whole.

The extent to which the culture to which you subscribe is individualistic or collectivist will influence your relationships with others. It will influence the amount of emotional (and sometimes material) dependence that group members have on one another. It will influence the extent to which individual needs are balanced against group needs and whether rewards are allocated individually or to groups.

According to Hofstede's research, those who subscribe to an individualistic culture tend to:

- Be more independent of their employing organisation.
- Defend their personal or leisure time more strongly.
- Demand more freedom and scope in their job.
- Want more autonomy.
- Prefer to make decisions individually rather than collectively.
- Pursue their own needs and ambitions with less regard for others' needs.
- Consider that they are responsible for looking after themselves.

Those who subscribe to a collectivist culture tend to:

- Prefer to work for large, more established organisations.
- Be more morally committed to and involved with their organisation.
- Take others into account more often and to a larger extent.
- Prefer group decision making and consider what's best for the group.
- Believe that if they help the group, the group will look after them.

Implications for trainers

- In a highly individualistic culture learners will be interested in individual reward schemes. These might be bonuses for completing a course, learning how to give their staff personal rewards for high individual performance, or appraising and assessing staff on an individual performance or merit basis.

- In a collectivist culture a training programme related to installing a reward scheme for individuals is unlikely to be well received. It is counter culture. People will see it as inappropriate, unworkable and unwanted because it threatens one of their core values and beliefs.

  They would probably prefer a scheme that rewards group or team performance, or else an equal distribution of profits to all members of the group. If one member of a group is perceived as not doing their fair share people in a collectivist culture tend to deal with the problem by using group or peer pressure.
- Individual objectives are usually most appealing to an individualistic culture, but group or team objectives are likely to appeal to a collectivist culture.
- Learners who subscribe to an individualistic culture often like to learn about such areas as: achieving freedom, autonomy, individual decision making, asserting individual needs, having personal learning needs met, putting over a personal point of view, earning promotion and individual pay increases.
- Learners who subscribe to a collectivist culture are more likely to want to learn about such ideas as: carrying their whole team with them, achieving corporate objectives, doing what's best for the section or organisation, meeting group needs even if those are different from their own personal hopes, and getting their whole group's views and needs met.

Masculinity/femininity

Hofstede's fourth dimension categorises culture as either having predominately 'masculine' or 'feminine' perceived characteristics. When following Hofstede's work it is important to understand that he uses the term 'masculinity' to refer to characteristics such as assertiveness, and 'femininity' to describe nurturing behaviour. He does not mean that all men are assertive and all women nurturing!

Hofstede's analysis shows that a culture that is high in 'masculinity' tends to emphasise assertiveness, advancement, freedom, recognition, independence and technical or logical decision making. A culture that is high in 'femininity' tends to emphasise working atmosphere and conditions, cooperation, concern for others, relationships and decision making that includes the use of intuition.

Implications for trainers

- If in your organisation the training department's culture is seen to be nurturing (feminine in Hofstede's terms) and senior management culture is seen to be 'masculine', will the training department's proposals and ideas be listened to? Will the training department be respected and be seen to have value and credibility? Senior management may perceive the training department as basing its proposals and decisions on inappropriate methods, values and circumstances. People in the training department may see senior management in a similar way.

- On a training programme many trainers set up a nurturing culture to help people to learn. Often the programme works well as a result of that supportive culture. However, learners are not usually prepared for a difference in culture on their return to work – and sometimes the culture back at work will be a masculine culture. Learners are not prepared for the differences in values, assumptions and beliefs and can become quite disillusioned and demotivated as a result.

- You may have been asked by senior management to increase cooperation between departments, train people through team building, build networks and relationships: that is, help to build a more feminine culture. However, the structures that are in place may be primarily designed to support a masculine culture: for example, rewarding and emphasising individual assertiveness or personal advancement. As a trainer you will experience many blocks, barriers and frustrations with the learning event and in terms of helping learners to transfer the learning back to work unless the structures are changed to support team building, cooperation between departments and networking as well.

Let's examine now some case studies which involve trainers and learners with different values and beliefs.

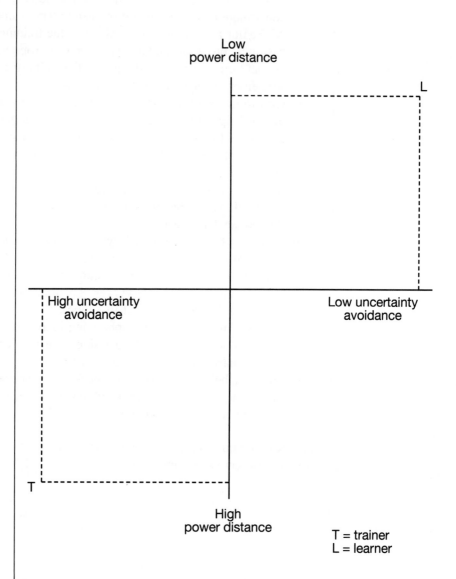

Diagram 6. Trainer/learner culture: case study 1

This case study describes a trainer who prefers to subscribe to a culture of high power distance (that is, the trainer having more power than the learner) and high uncertainty avoidance (that is, prefers to avoid uncertainty). The trainer prefers to:

- Tell learners exactly what to do.
- Run a rigid preplanned programme.
- Allow few or no variations.
- Use exercises that have predetermined outcomes and right answers.
- Deliver set lectures and inputs that can be substantially, if not totally, preplanned.

The learner in this case study subscribes to a very different culture – low power distance and low uncertainty avoidance. The learner prefers to:
- Be equal in terms of power and control.
- Have their ideas and suggestions taken into consideration.
- Have some say in issues even if they appear insignificant, such as when to have a tea break, or how long to take to complete an activity.
- Take risks.
- Experiment with ideas.
- Be more open-ended over outcomes.
- Explore issues which arise even if time for those issues has not been timetabled. Learners can become very frustrated if they cannot do this, especially if the issue is directly relevant to the learning outcomes or objectives.

So if both the trainer and the learner continue to act in their preferred way there is likely to be considerable conflict in terms of communication, understanding and expectations.

Case study 2

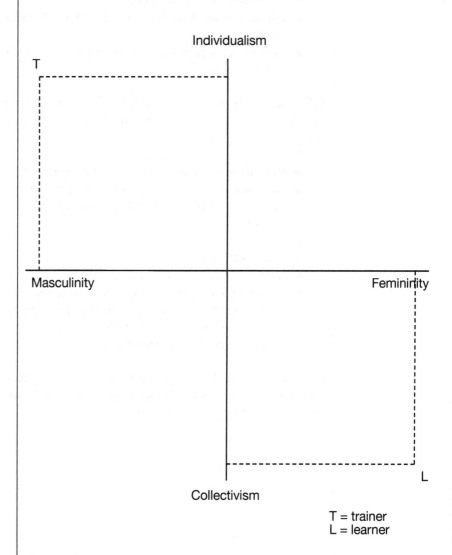

Diagram 7. Trainer/learner culture: case study 2

Before turning to the details of this case, look at the dimensions for the trainer and learner and try to imagine their cultural preferences.

What sort of problems and conflicts might they experience if they are strongly entrenched in their views and not prepared to give way? This study represents an actual case known to the authors which met this pattern.

In this case the trainer was frequently known to say: 'Take responsibility for your own learning. Further your own development through your own self-determination: Never mind about what others are doing, look after yourself.' He was very keen to encourage people to be heard, put forward their views assertively and have their views recognised. If someone had made a good case for receiving certain training he made sure that they got it, but he did not tend to ensure that others in similar circumstances benefitted too.

The learner in this case study came from a culture in which nurturing, coaching, gentle guidance and support were greatly valued. A team approach was important; all members, including the less assertive, were looked after so long as they made a fair contribution to the team.

This learner perceived the trainer as aggressive, and saw his approach as uncaring for the less able, as one which would divide teams and generate unhealthy competition rather than build cohesive groups.

The trainer perceived the learner as:

● Weak.
● Unrealistic because he was looking for solutions which would meet not just his own personal needs, but the needs of all his team members at work as well.
● Wanting too much direction and support.
● Afraid to voice his own opinion if it was likely to be different from that of the rest of the group.

The following case study shows how on a particular learning event the trainer perceived the learners. There were four learners, indicated by L1 to L4, and the trainer, indicated by T. The learning event was a train-the-trainer one-day workshop.

The diagram below represents the cultural dimensions of the learners and the trainer as perceived by the trainer during a train-the-trainer workshop.

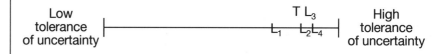

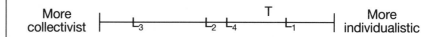

Diagram 8.   Trainer/learner culture: case study 3

Some of the more interesting issues which arose in this group were:

- The trainer and the learners felt comfortable sharing experiences and ideas and with learning from each other. The trainer was not expected to have answers to every problem. (Low power distance for trainer and learners.)
- Learner L1 needed more guidance, support and structure in order to participate and in order to experiment with the ideas discussed. L1 was afraid of uncertainty and taking risks. (Lower tolerance for uncertainty.)

    L1 had a similar problem at work. L1 was afraid of losing control and afraid of unknown reactions and questions from the group. To 'solve' the problem L1 talked continuously giving no opportunity for unexpected questions. But, it did not help L1's learners to learn in the way they needed to and L1 felt unhappy about this.
- Learner L3 came from the voluntary (charitable) sector and a culture which emphasised cooperation, group decision making and meeting group needs rather than individual needs only. The trainer, who came from a more individualist culture, and who mainly worked with learners from individualist cultures, had to make a conscious effort to relate to and meet L3's needs. (Collectivist/individualistic dimension of Hofstede's work.)
- When it came to discussing and developing styles and methods of debriefing and reviewing learning activities during this train-the-trainer workshop, learners L2, L3 and L4 all subscribed to a more nurturing culture (and so did the trainer). It would have been very easy for the trainer to fall into the trap of condemning L1 as being 'wrong' because L1's culture was more 'masculine'. Instead the trainer had to probe more deeply to understand L1's needs in this area.

For trainers

Four dimensions of an organisation

Purpose

This activity is designed to provide practice in applying Hofstede's four dimensions of culture to an organisation you know well. It is intended to improve your familiarity with terms and concepts used in relation to Hofstede's work on culture.

Method

- Describe an organisation which you know well in terms of Hofstede's four dimensions. Write down examples of each dimension and reasons why you think the organisation is high or low on each dimension.
  The four dimensions are:
  - Power distance.
  - Uncertainty avoidance.
  - Individualism/collectivism.
  - Masculinity/femininity.
- What are the training implications? For each dimension write down at least one issue that is relevant to the organisation you have analysed. The purpose of this is not to stereotype the organisation but to note down what points you would check as a result of analysing the organisation in relation to the four dimensions.

Debrief

- To what extent is the culture of this organisation similar to or different from the culture you subscribe to?
- What issues will you have to address as a result of these similarities and differences?

Conclusion

This type of analysis can give you a new insight into some of the common problems and issues which trainers and learners face. It helps to explain some of the apparent mismatches and some of the frustrations which people have to cope with.

With this knowledge in hand you are in a better position to recognise some of the issues and so adopt a more constructive approach towards reaching an effective solution.

For trainers

Different cultures – one organisation?

Purpose

The purpose of this activity is to help you explore the cultural differences of different parts of an organisation using Hofstede's dimensions as a tool for analysis.

Method

- Select two or three different areas or parts of an organisation. Ideally choose sections which are as different as possible (for example, in terms of function or geographical location).
- Talk to the people in those sections by telephone, visit them if you can and use any other ways of gathering information about the culture of each of your chosen sections.
- Note down where you feel each section lies in terms of the four dimensions. Make a comparison study between the sections. Are there big differences in the culture? Are there strong similarities in some dimensions?

Debrief

- If there are significant differences in culture between the different sections, why do you think this is? After all, they are all part of the same organisation.
- If there are strong similarities in culture between the different sections, what do you feel has helped to achieve this?
- What are the implications for training?
  - For each section on its own?
  - When mixing people from different sections?

Conclusions

Be careful about stereotyping. Hofstede's dimensions are useful but they do not represent the whole picture.

Also, within any one section there may be wide individual differences, so this analysis will be useful in understanding general trends and tendencies only. It can be valuable if you need to make decisions about how next to help large numbers of learners from an organisation on a group basis.

Some organisations prefer to spread their values and beliefs strongly throughout the whole organisation, no matter where branch offices may be situated in the world. They believe that one approach is right, or certainly the best that can be done in a given situation. However, it often happens that national or regional cultures prevail over an organisation culture. Some difficult problems arise when trainers try to use the same training methods for different cultures without regard to regional or national culture. Anything from obvious disregard to quiet withdrawal, from strikes and unrest to subtle and covert adaptation to suit their needs, can occur as a result either during the learning event or afterwards.

Activity 11

Learner/workplace culture

Purpose

This activity is designed to explore the differences between the culture of a particular learner and the culture of the section in which they work. The aim is to assess the implications of culture for the learning process in relation to an individual learner.

Method

- Take three or four people you are helping (on the same learning event if possible). Describe them in terms of Hofstede's four dimensions both on the basis of what they have told you and from what you have observed.
- Try to describe the culture of the section in which each of them works in terms of the four dimensions. Try to find out about the culture of each learner's section from a range of sources.

Debrief

For each learner:

- What are the differences, if any, between the culture that the learner appears to subscribe to and the culture of the section for which the learner works?
- What are the implications for the learning and development process for each learner?

Conclusion

The following are some of the issues which can arise:

- Where there is a difference between the learner's culture and the culture of the section in which the learner works, the trainer can plan for those differences to be taken into account. This is especially important in terms of how the learner is going to implement personal learning points.
- Where there are similarities that are strengths in terms of what needs to be achieved, then the learner can be helped to identify and build on those factors.
- Where there are similarities that hinder or block progress then you can allocate some time to those issues. Simply ignoring those issues is unlikely to help. The training is unlikely to be effective and may, in fact, do more harm than good.

Summary

One way of describing a culture is in terms of Hofstede's four dimensions:

- Power distance.
- Uncertainty avoidance.
- Individualism/collectivism.
- Masculinity/femininity.

National or regional culture can be a strong influence and can sometimes override attempts by multinational organisations to establish a common culture throughout the organisation.

It is helpful for trainers to recognise where they are in terms of each dimension and where their learners are. Use Diagram 9 to help you. Frustrations can occur because of a mismatch on these dimensions. Some key cultural issues include:

- The trainer having the 'wrong' leadership style.
- The degree of participation expected by the trainer and needed by the learner.
- How comfortable learners are with particular methods of learning, such as lectures, self-managed learning, role play.
- How willing the trainer and learners will be to experiment or take risks.
- How much the trainer and learners rely on set procedures and rules to guide their behaviour.
- How much freedom, autonomy, and individual decision making is expected.
- The extent to which nurturing or assertiveness is expected.

For a group of learners on a course or learning event which you are leading, plot each learners culture in terms of the four dimensions. Also plot your own culture, and that of any co-trainers.

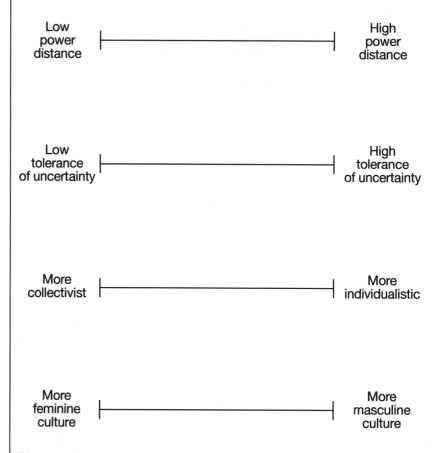

Low power distance	High power distance
Low tolerance of uncertainty	High tolerance of uncertainty
More collectivist	More individualistic
More feminine culture	More masculine culture

Diagram 9. Plotting trainer/learner cultures

Part III — Culture and the learning event

Introduction to Part III

The structure of Part III reflects the cycle of a learning event starting from writing the advertisement, through icebreakers, main activities, debriefing and review. Each chapter contains some ideas on how culture can influence the learning and development process. As in the rest of this book there is a mixture of concepts, ideas and practical activities.

Throughout Part III we shall be linking conventional approaches with the implications of culture.

6 | Advertising literature

Whether you work within a company as an internal trainer or externally as a consultant you will often need to advertise the learning events or help you are offering. Many companies produce a booklet listing the courses on offer, with details of individual events, their duration and who they are designed for. Other organisations produce advertising literature to publicise each learning event. Whatever you decide to do your product will create its own image in the eyes of your potential learners and will help people to decide whether or not to take part (and managers to recommend/decide who should be nominated).

The course flyer or advertising literature for a learning event gives you an opportunity to say something about the culture to which you as the trainer subscribe. It also provides a chance to indicate the cultural background of the person who might wish to apply for the event. Bear in mind that it must follow best practice, organisational policy and legal requirements in terms of issues such as discrimination, equal opportunities and business ethics.

The literature can be used to target training so that only certain groups apply. For instance, if you want to develop people who will find the concept of empowerment acceptable, then making the word empowerment prominent in the advertising literature will help to attract people from a culture in which that concept is seen as positive. It may also attract people with opposite views who might seek to challenge or sabotage the event. Suitable screening can help to alert you if this is happening.

It is important to visualise the type of people you are targeting and, just as important, the type of people you are not targeting. This applies not just to external course providers but also to internal training departments who have to work within self-financing guidelines. This approach helps ensure the quality of a learning event. After all, you want to reach people for whom the learning event is appropriate.

Trainers often spend enormous amounts of time designing a learning event but usually very little on designing the flyer or advertising literature.

One of our colleagues told us this story: 'Recently when I had to design some advertising literature for a programme I found there were some interesting analogies with a catering course my mother attended at a local college. At the college they spent a considerable amount of time teaching the students about the presentation of food. I've always remembered the sequence of importance that they taught.

'Firstly, the most important thing to get right in the eyes of the customer is the description of the food. This description is usually the deciding factor on what food they order. The next most important aspect is the look of the food as it is brought to the table and placed on the plate. At this stage the customer will confirm that they are satisfied with what they ordered. The next item of importance is the smell. And finally there is the taste – the consumption of the product.'

He continued his story by saying 'If all the previous steps are accomplished to the customer's satisfaction, then the consumption is almost a foregone conclusion and only something significant, like a 'hot' meal served lukewarm or cold, will cause dissatisfaction. So, whereas you might expect the eating of the food to be the most important issue, it is actually the least important because if the other areas are wrong then the customer will either end up not ordering the food or will have decided beforehand that it is not going to be a superb meal. In much the same way, the 'consumption' of training is greatly influenced by the way in which it is offered, the way it is presented beforehand, the way in which it is advertised. If these preliminaries are not done well the learner may decide that it will not be a good product.'

Coming back to the analogy with food, it is not just the actual food that appeals to someone. Caterers and chefs go to great lengths to ensure that everything related to the dining process will appeal to the customer's needs right from the start. Take, for example, the wording of menus. Would you expect many people to order 'the pancreas or thymus gland of an animal'? It would probably appear on the menu as 'sweetbreads'. Or how about a mixture of 'pigs blood and minced pork fat' – the North of England product more commonly known as black pudding?

How does this link to culture and advertising learning events? Well, are you advertising 'black pudding' or 'pig's blood and minced pork fat'? What is meaningful and acceptable to the culture of your intended learners? Sometimes there is a case for being direct, and sometimes for dressing up the subject. You need to make a conscious decision. After all, if the learners or their managers are basing their decisions on the advertising literature they must like the look of what's on offer. If it's not packaged to their satisfaction then it won't appeal to them, even if it's based on properly assessed training and development needs and been tailored just for them.

But how *do* you package your event to the customer's satisfaction? Surely there are so many types of people around that any one advertising leaflet could not possibly cover them all. Well, our suggestion is that you do what the caterers do:

- Decide who your customers are.
- Decide what you want to offer them/what they need.
- Find out what is currently fashionable and acceptable to their culture(s).
- Write the flyer taking the above factors into account. You may want to produce different flyers for different groups.
- Remember to test your literature before the launch.

Smell may not be particularly appropriate to the type of training with which you are involved, but the description of it, the look and the consumption can certainly be tailored to your customers. Let's follow up some of these ideas in more detail.

Decide who your customers are

It is difficult to write advertising literature or a course description so that it will appeal to all cultural backgrounds. If your promotional material is going to be read by a very wide range of people then you need to decide who you particularly want to attract. Your answer could be based on people's positions in the hierarchy, such as junior, middle or senior management. It could be to do with certain skills learners possess, or need to possess, such as keyboard dexterity or the ability to use a certain software package. Or, you might want to reach learners with certain behavioural needs, such as assertiveness or self-esteem.

If you don't decide who your potential customers are you run the risk of not considering them at all. This can result in a bland, compromised approach, or one that appeals to a particular cultural grouping, but maybe not the one you intended to reach.

Decide what you want to offer them

Once you know who your customers are you need to know how you can help them. Are you offering knowledge to help them start on a particular learning path, or to enhance an area they are already familiar with?

Are you offering them a skill or set of skills so that they can tackle new or existing situations with more tools at their disposal? Are you offering an attitudinal alternative so that they can change their approach to events and situations? Learners and their managers will be looking at the flyer to see which areas your event can help them with. There will be learning areas and learning methods that will be seen to be 'not for them' or 'flavour of the month'. Learners in a particular group may have certain development needs but may not take up the offer if it is perceived as threatening or confrontational. Of course what is threatening and confrontational to members of one cultural group may be seen as acceptable by another group.

Working as an in-house trainer you have the advantage, if you can make use of it, of being able to find out what kind of learning events people in the organisation have experienced in the past. You may be in a position to discover what worked successfully and why. What was less effective and why? Through careful investigation you might also explore different reactions in different parts of the organisation to a particular learning event.

When you are investigating try to minimise assumptions you may have to make – or which you hear from others. All organisations contain people who make unhelpful stereotypical assumptions about different departments and sections. For example, 'We all know that everyone in the marketing department is extrovert and drinks heavily, don't we?' and 'all trainers live on another planet'!

When offering training solutions, of course, you must offer something that is of use and value, but you also need to take into account the culture. Should the advertising literature challenge the culture or should it go with the existing flow?

Finding out what is fashionable

Like most other subjects learning has its fads and fashions. And, as in other areas, fashions can very quickly change regardless of how useful they might be.

One example is the rise and fall in many countries of transactional analysis as a management development tool. In the late 1960s and early 1970s it was seen as *the* way to help people learn soft management skills, such as dealing with relationships. However, it was misused by many management trainers who simply earned themselves the reputation of being 'amateur psychologists'. Later other developmental tools, such as neuro-linguistic programming, became fashionable in their turn.

However, transactional analysis has become more popular again in the early 1990s as trainers have gained a more sophisticated understanding of how it can be used. It can be seen to serve such fashionable objectives as 'delegative management' and 'empowerment'.

Fashion is not only to do with what is trendy in training and learning techniques. It is also to do with what will fit the culture of the organisation concerned and what the training is trying to achieve. Some organisations will look at advertising material to seek learning experiences that fit with existing cultures, while others will be looking for learning that deliberately thrusts them into new areas. Yet other organisations will be looking for learning that moves away from existing cultures and encourages the learners to become managers of change.

The flyer or advertising literature need not give detailed information about the learning content and philosophy but should provide 'hooks' that attract those learners most in need of the event. An example of this was a 'Handling a Pressured Lifestyle' workshop which was actually a stress management workshop. To have advertised it as a stress management workshop would have frightened away the very people who needed it in a particular organisation. In that culture pressure was an acceptable word but stress was not.

Some trainers may regard this approach as akin to basic selling techniques – and it is. In order to help the people who most need it you must reach them in a way that is acceptable both to them individually and to the culture in which they operate. The specific selling technique we recommend is to consider the assumptions, values and beliefs of the cultures to which your learners belong when designing your advertising literature, in addition to all the other factors which you normally take into account.

Develop your expertise at writing effective advertising material by working through Activity 12.

For trainers

Writing advertising literature

Purpose

This activity is designed to give you practice at applying cultural considerations to the writing of advertising literature for learning events.

Method

- Choose a learning event for which you have to produce some advertising literature. It can be an internal, in-company programme, or a public workshop, depending on the kind of work with which you are involved.
- Apply a step-by-step approach to designing the material by:
  - Determining the type of people you want to reach.
  - Identifying 'hooks' that might be suitable for them. (To do this you will have to explore what is culturally acceptable for these groups.)
  - Clarifying what it is you are offering them. How does it meet their needs? How does it blend with their culture?
- If you have chosen at least two distinct groups that you want to reach try writing the advertising literature in a different way for each group.
- Test your literature on a sample audience if you cannot actually experiment with it.

Debrief

Find out what does and what does not appeal to learners, their managers, and other trainers. Is the literature giving the picture you intended? How did different cultural groupings react to it?

Conclusion

Writing effective advertising literature is a skill that can be developed.

It takes thought and practice and a willingness to explore the 'hooks' that are relevant to other cultures. Without effective literature many people in your organisation may be deterred from attending a learning event which they really need. Remember the 'pig's blood and minced pork fat'!

Summary

When writing advertising literature for a learning event, in addition to the usual considerations of grammar, clear wording and so on, remember to:

- Decide whether the literature is to complement house style or be deliberately different.
- Identify the people you want to reach and to whom you want to appeal.
- Use words and terms that mean something to your prospective customers – avoid unnecessary training jargon.
- Be clear about what it is you are offering customers.
- Research the 'hooks' that relate to the people who need the training most.

Bear in mind that your literature must follow best practice, organisational policy, and legal requirements in terms of issues such as discrimination, equal opportunities and business ethics. The way in which you offer it should be influenced by in-house current fashions or external fashions.

Any advertising literature will automatically reflect the culture to which you subscribe and will either appeal – or not – to members of particular cultural groupings. As far as possible, you should be conscious of what you are doing and use the opportunity to best effect.

7 | Application forms

The application form is rarely used to gather information about a learner's culture and as such is a missed opportunity. Traditionally it is just seen as the document that learners fill in when applying to attend a learning event and it invariably asks for ordinary details such as name, address and telephone number.

It is a significant opportunity to gain more information because learners and their managers tend to be conscientious about returning an application form. They realise that the chance of attending the programme is greatly diminished if they do not give these initial details to the event organiser. They may not be quite so conscientious about returning subsequent questionnaires and forms which they may not perceive to be essential or vitally important.

Of course there are some occasions where application forms are unnecessary and inappropriate, but where they are used let's determine how you can make the most of the opportunity.

Using a standard form

Many organisations, both internal and external, favour the use of standard application forms. Standard forms provide a sensible way of obtaining basic details about those who will be attending. Advantages of standard forms are that they:

- Are cheaper to print.
- Save design time.
- Are easier to administrate.
- Fit computerised systems more easily.

The disadvantages however are that they:

- Present a very bland image to the customer.
- Do not allow for the collection of information which is pertinent to that particular event except with a very wide and ambiguous statement such as 'any other details relevant to the event which you are attending'.

Designing your own form

Unless you are running a production line of events for very large groups and have decided not to focus on people as individuals, it can be worth designing the application form specially to fit a particular learning event. In that design you can include questions or headings which tell you a little more about the learners' needs and the culture in which they operate. It gives you an opportunity to learn a little more about your learners so you can work with them as individuals, taking account of their different circumstances.

An example of how useful this can be is told in the case that follows.

'I am a systems trainer and I remember attending a systems analysis course which was run by a prominent computer training company. At the time my job involved training users of new computer systems. The systems were developed in-house by "the experts" but the day-to-day training was done by myself, a non-technical but very competent and experienced user. I did not understand how the system was developed but I knew how to use it. Each time a system was changed or updated I had to train some three hundred users in how to use it for their day-to-day work.

'It was decided that I could broaden my outlook and my job if I developed some expertise in analysing user needs and producing user requirements specifications. It was suggested that I attend a course on the subject as part of my development. We noticed an advertisement for a suitable course. My learning objectives and the course objectives seemed an excellent match. I filled in the course application form with my manager's support and sent it off without any concerns.

'The form asked for my name, business address, telephone number, dietary requirements, type of accommodation required and my mode of transport. When I arrived on the two-week residential course I discovered that I was the only person there who was not already a computer programmer.

'The course designers had assumed that all the learners would be programmers moving up the ladder of their organisation. Not only did they not cater for a non-technical learner, they had also missed their opportunity to find out about me. They could have recommended an alternative or made me aware of the potential difficulties at the application form stage.

'The culture in which the course designers had previously worked did not allow a job progression such as mine. Their assumptions, values and beliefs did not allow for other routes of progression, nor did they allow themselves the chance to find out that mine was different.

'One simple question would have identified the issue. But instead, my fellow learners, myself and the trainers had a hard time of it during that course.'

Another trainer's experience of course application forms has a happier ending.

'When I write a course, or reshape an existing one, I do it to satisfy an identified need. (If you are not writing to meet an identified need then I suggest that you question why you are doing it in the first place.) When I was asked by senior management to produce a series of management courses I asked what it was that they sought to achieve. They told me they needed general management courses so that their junior and middle managers were better trained. Not a lot to go on!

'My next move was to do a considerable amount of probing and studying of the business plan, interviewing managers at all levels, investigating the skills they had already, the skills they appeared to need, and discussing the types of learning events they had previously attended. At the end I produced a framework of learning objectives into which I could slot the individual learning needs of each manager.

'So I was able to design a course application form for this range of management courses that asked for details about:

- The sort of problems or learning needs that were preventing them doing their jobs effectively.
- What opportunities they saw for the future.

'This information, in addition to more conventional details, allowed me to better prepare for the course. I could obtain an initial insight into some of the assumptions, values and beliefs they each had. I could check the assumptions, values and beliefs I had used when designing the course. There was a chance to prepare and plan and to follow up where more information was needed.'

Working from sparse information

The next very simple case demonstrates the dangers of only being able to obtain very sparse information about learners. Imagine we are running a course to enable people to drive fork lift trucks. The first application form to arrive is from a male who is Italian and aged 25. The second application form is from a female who is English and aged 19. When examining the basic details of prospective learners most people will start to make assumptions about their probable driving skills and issues that may arise on the course.

It is difficult to avoid stereotyping but we can minimise the possibility by adding supplementary questions to the application form that relate to the abilities, needs and skills of applicants. Some options from which you could choose for the fork lift truck driving course are given below:

- How many years' driving experience have you had?
- What type of licence do you hold?
- Please give details of your previous driving experience.
- If you have had any experience of driving fork lift trucks or similar vehicles, please give details.
- Under what circumstances will you need to drive a fork lift truck?

The next activity will give you an opportunity to apply some of these ideas to learning events for which you are responsible.

Activity 13

For trainers

Designing an application form

Purpose

The purpose of this activity is to give you practice at designing an application form which provides more details than is usual about the learner's culture and the context in which they are working.

Method

- Choose a learning event which you have designed or which you are very familiar with running.
- Write down what information about the learner and the learner's culture you would like know about before the learning event begins.
- Design a suitable application form. Remember to be selective in which questions you ask. Do not ask too many questions, and be careful not to be seen as threatening or intimidating.
- Pilot the questionnaire before you use it for the real event.

Debrief

- After you have used the form for the actual event reflect back and identify the questions that provided you with useful information.
- What else should be included?
- Is there anything that should be omitted?
- To what extent were you able to check your own assumptions, values and beliefs as a result of the information you obtained?

Conclusion

Using the application form in this way may well be new for you. If you study application forms used by other trainers and learning providers you will not find many examples which ask for information of this sort. It will take some practice but a well-thought-out application form can produce tremendous rewards for both learners and trainers.

Summary

The application form can be a valuable tool for finding out about the learner's culture. It can also be very helpful to you in planning and preparing for a learning event.

The objectives of the application form are:

- To register learners for an event.
- To ensure they are going to be attending the right event for their needs and circumstances.
- To find out information, including cultural information, that will enable you to customise the learning to their needs.

In order to achieve this:

- Use application forms that can be tailored to the particular learning event where possible.
- Select questions that give you information that directly relates to the learning event.
- Pilot the form by asking potential customers to complete it. See how relevant and helpful the information is. Make changes if necessary.
- When you receive the completed forms for a particular course check that you are going to be able to meet the learners' needs. If there is a mismatch then deal with it as soon as possible.

8 | Joining instructions

We are using the term joining instructions to refer to the papers that you send to a learner a few days, or sometimes weeks, before they are due to attend a learning event. These papers tend to be used as confirmation of the learner's registration and as a reminder for the learner as to when and where the event is to be held. Occasionally a questionnaire is added for the learner to complete before attending, but seldom is the opportunity used for anything else.

In this section we suggest some ways of maximising this opportunity, particularly in relation to cultural issues. Let's start by examining one manager's experience of receiving joining instructions.

Perceptions based on joining instructions

'I remember attending my first management course. I had only been a manager for a few weeks and so I was keen to learn and make a good impression. I was pleased to be offered a place on a course (which was not in-house) so soon. I felt the timing was ideal to enable me to learn the intricacies and skills of management. The description of the course objectives seemed to match my needs well.

'I didn't feel deterred by the blue form which I had to complete in triplicate to be registered and I duly received my joining pack from the training provider. It included:

- A map and instructions on how to find the training centre.
- A letter confirming all the details.
- A list of all the delegates' names, job titles and company names.
- A list of materials I would need to have with me.

- The training centre dress standards.
- The training centre rules.
- Details of the swimming pool, golf course, gymnasium, pool and snooker tables, and table tennis.
- A copy of the course programme.
- Details of some pre-course work I would need to complete.
- A list of places of interest that were close to the training centre, local walks and jogging trails.

'So how did I feel after receiving that lot? Firstly, I wasn't sure whether I was going on a training course or a holiday. Secondly, I felt daunted by some of the details I read. The list of participants with their job titles looked very impressive and I had strong feelings of inadequacy. It seemed I was to be in the company of very experienced managers. Also the training centre looked more like a stately home and the dress standards confirmed my suspicions (there were photographs of men wearing suits and ties for dinner).

'Later I wondered what the training providers were trying to achieve in projecting this grand image. To me it seemed intimidating.'

In the case just described, the training providers may well have appealed to those who were responsible for sending the learners on their course. Nothing wrong in that but they certainly had not taken into account people for whom this culture would seem alien. Was it important to the learning process?

Cultural implications of joining instructions

There are some interesting cultural implications here. When you are designing a learning event by all means set the scene for the type of culture you believe is appropriate – but make sure you communicate that to your learners before the decision to attend is taken. Otherwise you may find you are attempting to train some very uncomfortable learners who feel that they are in the wrong environment. That does not help your business or their learning.

For those responsible for placing learners on external programmes remember to check not only the objectives of the course, standard of training and facilities but also the culture and atmosphere, and the values and beliefs of the training staff.

When setting up a tailored programme, it's all the more important to understand the needs, values and beliefs of the learners. Often much time is spent on training needs analysis, designing well constructed activities, buying in videos and materials, but very little considering the values and beliefs held by the learners.

Using joining instructions more effectively

So how can you use joining instructions in a more fruitful way? You can use them to:

- Confirm to learners that they are registered.
- Give them practical details on where, when, how to get there, what to bring and so on.

and

- Convey an impression which allows learners to create more accurate and helpful ideas about their impending experience.

Learners will tend to make assumptions anyway. If you don't take this into account you will not be aware of the problems, fears, concerns and expectations they will bring with them. By recognising the fact you can design the joining instructions to be user-friendly, to create as true a picture as possible and to minimise misinterpretations and problems.

By this stage you may well know something about the learners – both from the event flyer (who did you design it for?) and from the course application. So use this information to design helpful joining instructions.

It may well be that you have to have a brochure printed a long time in advance and it would not be cost effective to change it each time. So make the most of the accompanying letter. Unless you are dealing with hundreds of learners for each occasion, with a little effort you can personalise the letter to acknowledge some of the information you have already learned about them as individuals.

For instance, if you are dealing with a person who has particular dietary needs then you can mention that you have made the necessary arrangements – it will be something less for the learner to worry about. If the brochure shows pictures of people in formal wear but you are happy for learners to dress casually on this occasion then say so. Show the learners that you have read and understood their application forms and that you acknowledge their needs.

The next activity, on designing joining instructions, will help to consolidate the suggestions we have given.

| **For trainers**

Joining instructions

Purpose

This activity is designed to increase your awareness of the effect of joining instructions in relation to the cultural images they portray.

Method

- Collect some different joining instructions for a range of courses. You may want to collect samples that concentrate on the same topic in order to make more appropriate comparisons.
- Write down your views of the culture, style and atmosphere in relation to the learning event for each set of joining instructions.
- Show the joining instructions to three or four potential attendees. Then ask them to describe the image of each learning event that has formed in their minds, in particular their assumptions about the style, atmosphere and culture of the learning event.

    In order to obtain as wide a view as possible, choose people who belong to different cultural groups. Be careful not to influence the results by giving your views first. Use open questions.
- Ask if there is anything else you could have put in the instructions that would have helped them?

Debrief

- Look for the similarities and differences in their views. What was it that caused these?
- How different were their views from your own? Why do you think this is?
- Make a list of the items that are helpful and those that hinder.

Conclusion

A person's cultural background will influence the way in which they read the same joining instructions. However, some designs are far more user friendly and better tailored to the groups they are intended to reach than others. Reassess the joining instructions which are sent out in relation to the learning events you are involved with.

Summary

The joining instructions confirm a learner's registration for a learning event. They also act as a reminder to ensure that learners arrive at the right place, at the right time, with the right materials.

The joining instructions also convey an impression which cause learners to make assumptions about their pending experience. They will often form a picture of the culture of the programme based on those assumptions. An accurate, helpful impression will tend to aid the learning process. An inaccurate or daunting one can mean that considerable learning time is lost as learners experience 'culture shock'.

You can influence the impression made by using carefully developed joining instructions, which not only deal with practical and administrative details but convey an appropriate picture of the culture.

Always be clear about what you are trying to achieve with joining instructions.

9 | Briefings and briefing notes

For the purposes of this chapter briefing notes mean:
Notes to aid the discussion between learners and their managers (or sometimes their mentors) to:

- Clarify the objectives the learner will seek to achieve by taking part in the learning event

and

- Show how the achievement of these objectives will help the individual and/or the organisation in the future.

Briefing notes themselves are a culturally based phenomenon. In most organisations they are, unfortunately, inadequate.

Briefing notes give us the opportunity as trainers to find out more about the assumptions, values and beliefs that learners are bringing to the learning event. They also give learners the opportunity to find out something of the assumptions, values and beliefs of the trainers or designers of the event, before attending. They can be a very powerful tool to improve the effectiveness of the learning process.

However, there are many culturally based assumptions in our definition of briefing notes which need to be explored before progressing further. The first question to be examined is why people attend learning events.

Why people attend learning events

The are many reasons for attending learning events. It is important that we understand some of them so we do not fall into the trap of making false assumptions about why learners are there. Each of the following reasons for attending a learning event is valid and acceptable in certain cultures but not in others.

Reward

Some organisations use learning events to thank employees for a 'job well done'. The event may well have little to do with an employee's current duties but more to do with its perceived status value. The location of an event in another country, perhaps with free travel and subsistence for the learner's family, can enhance the perceived value of the reward. In some cases it is expected that learners will take time off from the course to make shopping expeditions as part of their reward. For others simply being wined and dined is regarded as ample reward.

Punishment

Similarly some people may be sent on an event to emphasise a rule or mode of conduct that they have not adhered to. The event may be involved with teaching the basics of the area in which they have 'offended'. In some cases people are sent on a relevant learning event before the official disciplinary process is begun so that the organisation cannot be accused of not having done 'all that was reasonable' to help the employee.

Everybody goes

Some learning events are compulsory for all employees performing particular functions or at certain levels, in certain sections or indeed of the organisation as a whole, whether or not there is an individually identified need. In some circumstances this is to meet legislative requirements, sometimes it is for indoctrination purposes, sometimes it is done 'just in case'. On occasions it is designed to engender a company spirit.

To use up the budget

Some organisations base next year's budget on the amount spent in the current year. If the budget is not used up it is cut the following year. So in some cases it can work to a manager's advantage to use up all the training budget before the end of the financial year. This can lead to a rush of attendance at learning events in the last two or three months of the year. In this circumstance the choice of learning events simply depends on what is available for those dates.

'You might learn something'

This phenomenon is often to be seen at the annual performance appraisal, when the appraising manager decides to send an employee on a learning event as an experiment. The briefing discussion may well consist of the appraising manager informing an employee that they are to attend, that 'they might learn something which will help them in their jobs and they should attend with an open mind'.

To keep out of trouble

There are other reasons linked with appraisal. One is that three-quarters of the way through the year the appraising manager may realise that a particular employee has not received any training and development that year and that there will therefore be a blank in the 'training and development' section of the appraisal form. The manager then rushes to put the employee on the first available course in order to avoid being reprimanded by the personnel department, or a superior.

Sometimes a learning event is chosen to keep employees quiet so that they do not cause trouble by saying they are not being developed.

To achieve specific objectives

Many learners do attend learning events in response to clearly identified learning needs. These may be related to the organisation and/or the individual. The extent to which these objectives are explained to an individual varies, however, from very clear explanations to none at all. A culture in which it is not normal for learners to know why they are attending particular events often suffers from poor transfer of learning because the learners are not committed to the entire process.

To put it on their CV

Sometimes learners (or their managers) feel it is important to have a recognised qualification in their field of work for reasons of status. It may be considered vital to have attended an external course on the subject given by an expert. Learners feel it will give them credibility either internally or externally, or make them more marketable. In some cases

115

the learners may be quite expert in the topic but have gained their knowledge through their own studies and experience. From their point of view attending an external event completes the process officially.

To fulfil the annual training quota

For some organisations a key indicator of quality and success is the total number of employee training days per year. It is seen as important to maintain or exceed last year's record. It is relatively easy to produce favourable statistics when trying to meet recognised levels of quality as defined by a national or organisational procedure. It also provides easy and impressive sounding detail to give to shareholders in an organisation's annual report.

'You haven't attended this one'

There are those managers who take a menu approach to training and development. They look at a brochure or table of courses and simply pick the next one on the list for their subordinates, with little regard for training needs. Sometimes particular courses are linked with job levels regardless of individual need.

To see what it's like

Some people will be sent on a learning event to find out what the event is like so that the manager or trainer can decide who else the course may be appropriate for.

To obtain new ideas

'To gain new ideas' is a favourite reason given by trainers and researchers for attending learning events. They notice a new course in an area they are developing and attend to see what ideas they can use in their own work. Sometimes they regard it just as an opportunity to probe and draw out ideas from an expert and are not particularly concerned with the published objectives.

To get someone out of the office

116 Some people are sent to a learning event in order to get them out of the

office when particular decisions are being made. Sometimes it is to give colleagues a break from a difficult colleague, or as a way of placating a difficult person because an unpopular course of action has to be taken.

Thus although learners may attend learning events specifically to cover material to do with their jobs it is not always the case and such an assumption would be unwise. In producing briefing notes you need to consider all of these reasons (and others which you will have come across within your own organisation).

Why encourage briefings?

You may be encouraging briefings to take place for a number of reasons:

- To encourage boss/subordinate communication in relation to learning and development.
- To encourage attendance at learning events only in response to clearly identified learning needs (rather than for some of the other reasons mentioned).
- To encourage discussion about the true purpose of attending the learning event in question and to be able to share those reasons with the trainer later.
- To prepare the learner so as to derive maximum benefit from attending.
- To lay the foundation for measuring whether attendance was effective and worthwhile. To set the basis of evaluation.
- To determine what needs to be done to make sure that the learning helps to achieve the organisation's objectives.

As a result of a briefing you may be just trying to find out what the cultural values are, or you may be using the opportunity to change the culture. To make briefings more effective you may wish to write briefing notes for the boss and/or the learner.

Writing briefing notes:

- Find out the variations in what currently takes place by way of briefings.
- Check the organisation's business plan, particularly for any reference to human resourcing. Many organisations do not have written objectives but nevertheless objectives do exist in the minds of the leaders (few organisations continue to survive where there is no direction and aim) so you may have to probe.

- Check where learning events fit into the culture of the organisation (and into the different sections within it).
- Decide whether you are trying to strengthen existing culture or change it in some way.
- Construct the guidance notes for the briefing to help achieve your aim.

There are three main sections which you should consider.

- Information to help the manager.
- Information to help the learner.
- Guiding the learners and their boss/es through the process of the briefing itself.

The following list is intended to provide a guide on what could be included in the briefing notes. It is not an exhaustive list. Nor will all the ideas be suitable for all organisations, so you will need to make appropriate choices.

Information to help the manager

- Summary of the event together with event objectives, outcomes, methods used, opportunities.
- Prerequisites for attending under the headings of medical needs, physical requirements, knowledge needed, skills which must be attained before the learning event, opportunity for practice, previous experience, qualifications, language(s).
- Limitations of the event: sometimes it is important to say what is not covered.
- Time and resources: pre-course work, hours of attendance, evening work in the hotel or at home, post-course work, support to be provided by the manager or others, equipment or machines or computer access, books, videos.
- An indication of the type of special needs you as the trainer would like to know about: for example, learning needs, learning objectives, application areas.
- Mental preparation that the learner needs to do: for example, reviewing performance, considering potential areas of difficulty.
- The extent of course confidentiality:
  - Whether there will be any reporting back (if so in what form).
  - If there is to be any form of assessment.
  - What, if anything, will appear on the learner's official file.

You may want to ask the manager to prepare for the briefing by asking:

- How the learning objectives relate to the individual's job, either now or in the future.
- How the learning objectives relate to the section, and to the organisation's goals.
- For examples and evidence of the current gap in performance, if there is one.
- For examples and evidence of the new skills or behaviours which need to be developed.

You may like to include a copy of the briefing notes which you have given to the learner, or which you would like the manager to give to the learner.

Information to help the learner

You cannot be sure how much information, if any, has reached the learner. In many organisations information is given out in dribs and drabs, either deliberately or unconsciously. In some cases the manager does not see the issue as a high enough priority and does not bother with it – or only passes on some information the day before an event. There have been many events where we have found that learners have only been told the course title, plus where and when they are to attend.

So some of the choices you have in terms of the learner's briefing notes are:

- A summary of the event together with objectives, outcomes, methods used, opportunities.
- Prerequisites for attending under the headings of medical implications, physical requirements, knowledge needed, skills which must be attained before the learning event, opportunity for practice, previous experience, qualifications, language/s.
- The limitations of the event – sometimes it is important to say what it does not cover.
- Time and resources: pre-course work, hours of attendance, evening work in the hotel or at home, post-course work, support to be provided by the manager or others, equipment or machines or computer access, books, videos, what they need to bring with them.
- An indication of the type of special needs you as the trainer would like to know about: for example, learning needs, learning objectives, application areas.
- Details of the mental preparation that the learner needs to do: for

example, reviewing performance, considering potential areas of difficulty.
- Information on how the learning objectives relate to the individual's job, either now or in the future.
- The context: that is, how the learning objectives relate to the section's – and the organisation's – goals.
- The extent of course confidentiality:
  - Whether there will be any reporting back (if so in what form).
  - If there is to be any form of assessment.
  - What, if anything, will appear on the learner's official file.

The lists for the learner and the manager look remarkably alike and intentionally so!

However, some additional requests for information which you may like to add to the learner's briefing notes are:

- Their own personal learning objectives within the event objectives.
- The strengths and weaknesses, problems and opportunities they bring with them.
- Any particular ways in which they would like to be helped.

There may be special questionnaires, models or other tools that you can provide to help with this diagnostic process.

You may want to give the learner the opportunity to feed some issues back to you directly and confidentially and not necessarily though their boss.

Supporting the briefing process

You may want to provide learners and their bosses with a format or some guidance to help with the process of the briefing. If bosses are not used to conducting briefing sessions their uncertainty can lead to avoidance of the whole issue. They may have their list of questions but not know how best to conduct the session itself. For example, should the boss encourage the learner to give ideas first or should the boss lead the discussion?

The extent to which the guidance notes need to be prescriptive and directive will depend on the skills of the bosses in your organisation, the extent to which you need to encourage a common approach, and the extent to which you are trying to promote a particular set of values and beliefs. It will of course also depend on the prevailing culture in the organisation.

With some events you may know the learners, their bosses and the cultures in which they operate and you may be able to give more specific help. The information which we have covered so far will help you to decide what areas you need to help them pay special attention to.

In other situations you may know little or nothing about the learners and their cultures, and there may not be an opportunity to change that. In these cases you might choose to give a fairly wide brief that is sufficiently flexible to be adapted to different cultures. It is also important that you get back more specific information to help you to plan and prepare.

Summary

Culture is an important aspect of the briefings and briefing notes stage of the learning and development process.

- There are many reasons why people attend learning events – not all are to do with learning.
- Briefing notes can help to consolidate and support existing cultures or to facilitate change.
- Briefings can help the boss and the learner to recognise the assumptions, values and beliefs held by the trainers. They can do this by discussing the pre-course literature which has been issued or by considering any briefing they might have had from the trainers.
- Briefings can help the trainers to recognise the assumptions, values and beliefs held by the bosses and the learners.
- You may need to do some research before designing briefing notes.

10 | Pre-course work

Pre-course work can be set for a number of reasons, such as to:

- Enable the learners to start from the same point when they attend a learning event together.
- Identify existing cultural issues which are influencing the learning process.
- Work through material which learners can tackle by themselves and which would be a waste of group time.
- Identify the relationship between issues at the learning event and issues in the workplace.
- Discover which aspects of a topic learners would like to explore further.
- Determine which applications learners would like to develop.
- Achieve a common understanding of the topic.

The two areas which we will explore in more detail here concern using pre-course work to:

- Help learners to work from a common understanding.
- Identify other cultural issues which influence the learning and development process.

Working from a common understanding

When organisations introduce new ideas or make substantial changes, the trainers often play a vital role in helping learners to develop a common understanding of the new concepts and why they are being introduced. Sometimes senior managers just provide an explanation of what the changes are. They see that as being sufficient for people to subscribe to. Indeed in some cultures this works well and may be all that is needed.

But in many cultures, and certainly in many Western European cultures, this direction from the top is not always sufficient to produce a shift in attitude and behaviour. To achieve a change it may be important for all the learners to see the new issues from the same cultural viewpoint. It becomes important for everyone to have a common understanding. There are at least two ways of achieving this common understanding.

Some trainers choose to make it an objective during the learning event when everyone is together as a group. An alternative is to provide the learners with common information prior to the learning event so they arrive with the process well underway. This method can leave more time for learners to concentrate on issues that can only be looked at effectively as a group.

As an example let's take the subject of assertiveness. Different cultures will perceive the definition and application of assertiveness in different ways. Such differences can result in strong debate at the start of a learning event about exactly what assertiveness is – a result that may have been intended by the learning event designers in the first place. One alternative is to start with an understanding of the subject via precourse work. So let's explore some pre-course work that could help achieve this.

The cultural background of the organisation may dictate that the learners work with the company definition of the word assertiveness. One way of achieving this is to send the learners some reading on the subject prior to the event. It could be in the form of a book, a set of specially tailored handouts or some journal articles.

Alternatively you may want to encourage debate on the definition of the term. You may want learners to rethink and challenge the existing definition and associated values and beliefs. To stimulate thought you can send reading material that reflects a range of different approaches and then invite the learners to debate their thoughts on each one at the start of the event.

Whatever you decide to do, remember that the learners will need time to read and digest the material so make sure you send it out well in advance. Also bear in mind that in some organisational cultures it may not be acceptable for learners to spend work time 'unproductively'. Reading may come into this category. In other cultures learners themselves may feel embarrassed at doing something which may be regarded as studious. If you do send out pre-course work tell your learners why it is important and how it will be used. You may wish to draw their attention to the implications if they do not complete the work.

An alternative but more time consuming form of pre-course work, is to ask the learners to investigate the subject for themselves. Take negotiation as an example. Some organisational cultures see Win/Win as the definition of successful negotiation.

A Win/Win is where both parties in a negotiation regard the outcome as one which meets their needs. Other cultures prefer a Win/Lose definition where one party tries to win at the expense of the other.

To ensure that you do not make assumptions about the learners' interpretation of the word (especially important when you have learners from diverse cultures) you can ask them to investigate the cultures of negotiation in their own work areas. They may need to find out what their part of the organisation sees as criteria for successful negotiating, or they may need to observe one or more actual negotiations to find out for themselves.

Having explored the meaning of the word in their area they are then in a position to debate and consider the definition which you may want to offer them (or which their organisation wants them to work towards). They will also see from first hand knowledge that although they attach a particular meaning to a term (in this case negotiation), the people they meet and deal with in the future may have a different perception and hence a different approach to the subject.

From your point of view as a trainer, by asking the learners to investigate their own understanding of a topic, you are able to recognise each learner's perceptions, assumptions, values and beliefs. You are then in a better position to work with those differences when running the learning event.

Identifying other cultural issues

Another area which is often worth exploring is that of the acceptable norms that surround a subject area in the learner's work environment. For example, in one organisation it may be normal for the staff to challenge the ideas of their senior management; in another organisation this may be seen as totally unacceptable behaviour. This particular issue would probably be decided by the culture of power or authority.

These norms may not be apparent from a cursory visit to an organisation as they rarely feature in any published set of rules or procedures. The acceptable behaviour will be apparent from the way people talk about their bosses and the way in which people make decisions.

In many cases it will take more than simple and direct questioning to discover norms as the people concerned may be unaware of how and why they resolve issues in certain ways. Their awareness of the cultural norms is very often at a subconscious level. You may hear people say that the reason they try to do jobs well for their boss is to convey respect, or 'because they are my boss'. However, the evidence you see sometimes indicates other reasons such as fear of making mistakes. Fear can be a truer but much more hidden norm.

Concentrate your attention on the behaviours which people exhibit and the feelings that accompany them. Then, perhaps with the aid of someone with direct knowledge of these behaviours and feelings, you can begin to understand the cultural norms of an organisation.

Summary

Pre-course work can enable the learners to develop a common understanding of the concepts to be covered in the learning event.

Alternatively it can be used to identify learners' different perceptions of a subject based on the cultures in which they work. As a trainer this can help you to recognise and work with those differences.

It is sometimes useful to ask learners to examine the existing culture so that you can allow for variations in working practice. This can be very important in addressing issues relating to transferring the learning to the work place.

Careful study can enable your learners to identify that cultural norms apply in their work place, some of which are a help, others of which are a hindrance to the learning and development process.

11 | Pre-course questionnaires

This chapter will outline some of the ways in which pre-course questionnaires can be used, especially in relation to the implications of culture on the learning and development process. Many trainers send out pre-course questionnaires either after learners have been nominated for a particular learning event or with the joining instructions. Much of the information will also be helpful if you use questionnaires as an integral part of a learning event as well as a pre-course tool.

Psychometric tests

To many people in the human resources field the word questionnaire conjures up images of psychometric tests. The use and accuracy of psychometric tests is not a subject covered in this book; there is much written by the experts already. We simply mention them as an option you may wish to consider in order to help your learners understand themselves better and to help improve your understanding of the learners and the issues they face.

In our experience an appropriate psychometric test will help you find out an enormous amount of information that will enable you to identify some of the cultural values to which your learners subscribe. If you wish to follow up the use of psychometric tests we recommend you obtain advice from an expert in the field.

Questionnaires

We will now go on to explore other types of questionnaires, under the following headings:

- Questionnaires and the learner.
- Questionnaires and relationships.
- Questionnaires and how the learner works.

Questionnaires and the learner

In addition to psychometric tests there are other standard questionnaires that you can send to learners before they attend a learning event. Questionnaires can cover such areas as:

- The learner's personality (through processes such as transactional analysis).
- The learner's preferred methods and styles of learning.
- The learner's behaviours.
- The learner's skills.
- The learner's knowledge of various subjects.

When deciding whether to use a questionnaire clarify in your own mind the following points:

- The type of learning event.
- What you know about the learners already.
- What you would like to know about the learners.
- What you would like the learners to understand about themselves before the learning event.
- Whether this is a case where a questionnaire would produce information of quality in a cost effective way.

Compare your answers with what the various questionnaires on the market can achieve. Try not to compromise by using a questionnaire that only partly meets your needs. Parts which learners perceive to be irrelevant can demotivate, frustrate or irritate them.

In addition to scanning the market for existing questionnaires you can obtain help from a consultancy or research organisation; they will create a questionnaire that is tailor-made for your needs. Or you can design a questionnaire of your own. This last option is not as daunting as it may sound: remember you may only need a simple questionnaire not a full-blown psychometric test.

If you decide to design your own questionnaire follow some simple guidelines:

- Check your questions for bias.

- Keep the questions as simple and jargon free as possible.
- Keep the number of questions as low as possible.
- Pilot the questionnaire to make sure the questions are clear and unambiguous, and that they produce the results you need.

Because we subscribe to different beliefs and values, issues that one person may see as fundamental to a topic may be completely immaterial to another. The job of managing these differences on a learning event can be made a little easier and more productive if you can identify some of these values and beliefs.

Sometimes you may feel that a questionnaire is the most appropriate way of obtaining this information. At other times you may prefer to conduct an interview or discussion, send out pre-course assignments or run an exercise during the learning event.

Questionnaires and relationships

'Personality' questionnaires do not usually identify cultural differences but concentrate on what is different about the individual's personality. It can be a good starting point for identifying why two people are different but may not necessarily show you how they behave or think as a result of those differences.

It is unlikely that personality questionnaires will tell you about the influence of culture. In fact, you can find two people with very similar personality profiles who would relate to a third person in a very different way even in the same circumstances. Two important factors accounting for these differences are the experiences the people have undergone and the different values and beliefs they subscribe to.

Take care! Do not allow yourself to start stereotyping people because of their personality types and so make assumptions about their values, and beliefs and how they will behave. One benefit of using personality tests is that they remind us that our learners are different from us. Just because we see things in a certain way, or relate to others in a certain way, does not mean that they will.

Other types of questionnaires that concentrate on relationships examine differences in approach to various issues, such as working in a team or boss-subordinate relationships. They examine how a learner behaves – or perceives how they behave.

If you take management style as an example, it can be very useful to obtain a learner's perception of current style. You can then relate that to the culture in which the learner works. Where the management style is seen as contrary to cultural norms, is the learner perceived as someone who is innovative and forward thinking, or as an ineffective person who is trying to rock the boat? Where the learner's style is consistent with cultural norms is that person seen as entrenched and not moving with current demands, or as a 'good manager with development potential'? Such insights can make a huge difference in the way you might plan and design a learning event.

Questionnaires and how the learner works

Other kinds of questionnaires examine the style and method the learner actually uses in the work place. They are outcomes-based and so are usually concerned with the collection of data. The type of data will depend on the objectives of the learning event. Time management makes a good example.

One well-known approach to time management is to encourage learners to find out how they currently use their time – based on real data and not just their perceptions. Questionnaires and time logs are given to the learners to complete as they go through two or three typical work days. To achieve a balanced assessment they can ask their boss, secretary, assistant or colleague to fill in the questionnaire and time log as well. The learners can then consolidate the information and give it to the trainer before the learning event.

The data in itself will not tell you about the culture in which the learners work, or the values and beliefs to which they subscribe, but it will give you the information on which to base your follow-up questions. If, for example, you discover that most of the learners in a particular section frequently work an hour or so after their staff have left, your follow-up questions concern whether this behaviour is based on actual workload, or based on their culture's way of showing that a person is hardworking and therefore worthy of promotion? You can decide whether to follow up before or during the learning event.

Without this knowledge you may be wasting considerable time and effort helping your learners to find ways of leaving work earlier which they have no real intention of putting into practice because they want their next promotion! Identifying, acknowledging and working with cultural differences is not easy but some of this pre-course input can make the learning and development process far more effective.

Summary

Pre-course questionnaires may involve psychometric tests but that is only one aspect of the subject. Many other questionnaires are straightforward documents designed, issued and analysed by a professional trainer who is not necessarily qualified in psychometric testing or psychology.

If you are going to use psychometric tests we recommend that you obtain help and advice from a qualified practitioner.

Some questionnaires will provide information about personality, others about working relationships and others data on working practices.

You can use a questionnaire as your starting point to find out information relating to culture and its implications on the learning and development process.

12 | Icebreakers

Icebreakers have been a ritual at many learning events for some years now. Many trainers use them as a way of setting the group at ease, helping people relax and talk to each other and to break the ice. There are many very effective activities which help to do just that. But let's examine how icebreakers can also be used to help with the effects of culture on the learning and development process.

Using icebreakers

Consider the position of a learner about to join one of your learning events. Some learners may only have been able to judge the pending experience from the various communications they have had with you and, perhaps, by talking to someone who has attended a previous programme. But has any of this helped them? It is hoped that they will have received from you some specific information on which to base their perceptions but discussions with a previous learner may or may not have helped.

Take, for example, a learning event which is very responsive to individual learners' needs and which is tailored to fit a particular group. This could mean that although a series of learning events is run under the same name and same published overall objectives the actual experience, range of activities, tutor inputs, style and approach may be very different. Consequently each time the event is run it will be different and the learners may well have heard that this is the case.

This is in stark contrast with other types of learning events which run under the same name and same published objectives and in more or less the same way each time. Learners may well have arrived with expectations based on what they have heard from previous attendees.

So here we have learners arriving at your learning event, each one with a set of hopes, fears and concerns based on their own previous experiences of learning. For some learners previous learning at school may be foremost in their minds; for others it may be a more recent event – good or bad. Each one is armed with their own cultural survival kit for use in unfamiliar or uncomfortable situations.

Learners have told us that typical thoughts at this stage include:

- Will I be videoed?
- What will other learners/trainers think of me?
- Are other people here more advanced than me?
- Will I fit in with the group?
- Is there going to be anything which I can use back at work?
- What reporting back will there be?
- What if I'm no good at it?

On arrival learners usually go through a process of weighing up the other learners and the trainer. They form impressions about the event based on the surroundings and the welcome they receive.

This often unconscious process enables the learner to choose a set of behaviours that, in their cultural experience, will be acceptable to them and the rest of the group. These behaviours are used until they get to know the others better and can reassess the situation. The information they receive will be compared with their existing knowledge and experiences and the assumptions that result will determine how they behave.

If you decide to miss out the icebreaking activities for some reason – you are short of time, the course was late in starting or dinner took too long, for example – you will be in danger of a false economy because learners will be taking mental time out of the first sessions to go through the process anyway. (If this happens it is usually a longer and more difficult process for learners.)

Unknowingly learners will be wary of each other and this wariness is likely to disturb their concentration on the learning. If it is important that learning takes place as a result of working in groups, holding discussions, learning from and supporting each other, then it is vital to spend some time letting learners find out about each other and the trainer in a positive and constructive way.

For many trainers icebreakers serve to set learners at ease, create some interest in the learning event and let people introduce themselves. While these needs are very relevant icebreakers can also serve to provide yet more information about culture and how it is likely to influence the effectiveness of the learning process.

134 More detail is given about different kinds of icebreakers under three main headings:

- Icebreakers and the learner.
- Icebreakers and the learner's perceptions.
- Icebreakers and the learner's needs.

Icebreakers and the learner

Traditionally many learning events are started by the trainer asking each person to say a few words about themselves: such as, their name, what they do, where they work, their interests, and so on. This is all fairly safe information but nevertheless it enables the trainers and other learners to start making sense of the situation.

Although it probably is not their intention, trainers who run this type of icebreaker are actually attempting a basic sort of analysis of individual cultures, even if as a result they still treat everyone in much the same way. If you now start a similar icebreaker, with the awareness of the impact and implications of culture for the learning and development process behind you, you will see how useful this same icebreaker can be. It is brief and very simple in process, but it can provide you with some good starting points for identifying cultural issues.

For example:

- The hobbies and interests learners describe might indicate an enjoyment of, and comfort with, risk taking.
- The way in which learners spend their work and spare time may tell you whether they have preferences for being individualistic or collectivist (see Hofstede's dimensions on pages 59–67).
- The way learners present their information may indicate how comfortable they are in new situations and surroundings.
- The way the group reacts to what a learner says may tell you whether others seem to share norms or whether there are some contrasts.

But take care not to read too much into what is said. Remember that nervousness may mask some of the underlying issues. We are not suggesting that you should evaluate everything you see and hear – but it pays to be observant and recognise the similarities and differences.

Let's examine an icebreaker that is much more detailed than the example we have just given.

For learners

Picture me

Purpose

This activity enables learners to introduce themselves to each other and to the trainer. It enables the trainer to examine the background of each learner and gain a better understanding of the culture of that learner. It also enables the trainer to take the values and beliefs of each learner into consideration during the course or learning event.

Timing

You can use this activity as an icebreaker at the beginning of a course or learning event.

Materials

A piece of flipchart paper and a flipchart pen for each learner.

Time

40 minutes for a group of up to 12 learners.

Group size

Up to 12 learners.

Method

Explain that the purpose of the activity is for everyone to get to know each other in an informal way through drawing on a flipchart. Reassure them that artistic ability is not needed.

137   Give each learner a piece of flipchart paper and a pen and ask them to write their name on the flipchart.

Ask them to draw pictures of the main situations, places and people that have influenced their lives so far and be ready to explain and describe their flipchart to the others. The flipchart is not intended to be self-explanatory just an aid to their explanation.

Explain that they do not need to be good at drawing and that very simple pictures, symbols or diagrams can be used. Tell them that it is not their artistic ability that is being measured. Allow ten minutes for this. Be careful not to alienate anyone who may find drawing too threatening or unacceptable, let them illustrate themselves in another way if necessary.

The trainer(s) should also complete a flipchart.

Debrief

Encourage each learner to explain their flipchart. Learners and trainer(s) can ask questions about each other's pictures.

If you or another trainer, decides to go first a disadvantage may be that you may not learn as much as you might about the group because they are likely to copy your style and approach. However, an advantage is that it can show the learners that you are being open, prepared to take a risk and prepared to join in with everything that is going on. Learners may also feel less threatened because there is a role model to follow.

Conclusion

This type of activity is likely to encourage learners to be more open about their backgrounds. It provides the trainer with considerable information in relation to learners' assumptions, values and beliefs. It will not tell the whole story but it will give some important starting points. As a result you will be in possession of a considerable amount of cultural information, as well as having broken the ice, made introductions and started people talking to each other.

Additional information

This activity is particularly appropriate as an icebreaker on a programme which deals with interpersonal skills and personal development or empowerment. It will help to build up a 'trusting' and 'open' environment based on empathy with the individual and the culture of which they are a part. You should ensure that follow-on activities build on the trust and openness which has been developed. Helpful follow-on activities could be involved with setting objectives or assessing the skills, knowledge or applications they would like to develop.

Variations

- Learners could use words instead of pictures.
- The focus of the activity could be changed as follows:
    - Draw a picture of yourself in your job.
    - Draw a picture of the most significant moments of your life.
    - List the chapter titles of your autobiography.

Icebreakers and the learner's perceptions

We will now move on to explore icebreakers that can help achieve a clearer picture of the perceptions that learners have. These perceptions will be based on experiences in circumstances which they perceive to be similar or related to those that confront them now.

It can be very useful to know how learners perceive your learning event because their perceptions will strongly influence their expectations, hopes and fears regarding it and will have significant influence on the effectiveness of their learning process.

If you are going to offer learners something that is outside their expectations, or which has previously resulted in a 'bad experience', then you may need to manage carefully their introduction to this event. If their perceptions are not understood and not managed appropriately, learners are likely to adopt their cultural norms in handling what they see as threatening or difficult situations. Some of the most common reactions will be resistance, withdrawal and obstruction.

Training courses are/are not

This is an icebreaker which was used to start an interpersonal skills programme. The programme was for 11 learners from an organisation in the financial services sector. The learners, all of whom were at a managerial and professional level, were from three distinct backgrounds, namely, sales, systems and administrative support. Organisational constraints had not allowed for much pre-course contact with the learners and no briefings between the trainer and learners had taken place. (This is a situation which many trainers have to face in the course of their work.)

Most of the people did not know each other and many learners shared jokes about their experiences of learning events whilst coffee was being served on arrival. Picking up on these jokes the trainer decided that an icebreaker which consisted of a short self-presentation on key points, taking it in turns to go round the table, would not be welcomed.

Instead each person was given a piece of flipchart paper and asked to make two headings as shown in Diagram 10.

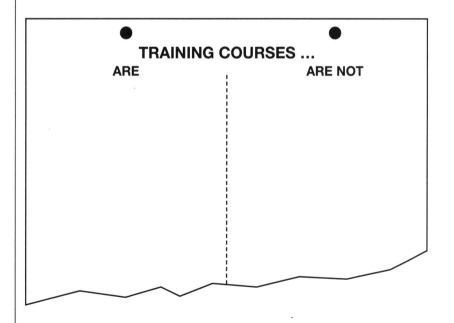

Diagram 10. Training courses are/are not

They were then asked to write down no more than ten comments that came to mind under each heading. The results were fascinating. In this particular case all the people from the sales section were very positive and saw training as an aid to their jobs. All the systems people saw technical training as essential but most had difficulty in seeing the relevance of behavioural training such as the interpersonal skills course they were now starting. Most of the administrative support managers saw training courses as a waste of time and were annoyed that they had been sent on this one: they had not volunteered to attend.

The net result showed that it was not a matter of saying that all sales people are like ... or all systems people think this ... but a matter of recognising that some people:

- Did not want to be there at all.
- Felt that training of this sort was not related to the real world.
- Could not see the relevance of behavioural training because they saw their managerial role as one of managing the tasks in hand, not one of managing the relationships involved in achieving those tasks.

It was useful for the trainer to be aware of the cultural norms prevailing in the different sections, to which most people subscribed. Some insight into the assumptions, values and beliefs behind those different reactions was important in planning the way forward. Considerable time might have been wasted by going straight into the first session without an ice-breaker; the differences in why learners were attending needed to be managed before any learning was likely to take place.

| # Using culture as the subject of an icebreaker

An introductory activity found to be useful in identifying learners' perceptions is one which concentrates on culture itself as the main theme. This can be particularly helpful if the learning event is culture related, such as one on customer care or quality management.

An icebreaker based directly on the subject of culture was used at the start of an event which aimed at effecting a cultural change in managerial approach. Fifteen learners from different geographical locations attended this five-day event. All they had in common was the fact that they all worked in the lower half of the managerial hierarchy of the same organisation. Most people knew someone else in the group, but nobody knew everyone.

The joining instructions had asked the learners to discuss their learning needs with their managers and to produce a list of objectives which they would like to achieve during the event. They had also been sent two questionnaires to complete before attending the event. The first concerned the way in which they preferred to learn, and the second their roles when working in a team. However, at the time of completion they were unaware of the exact way in which the questionnaires would be used.

At the start of the learning event the trainers introduced themselves and outlined the normal administrative details regarding the hotel, meals, telephone messages and emergency procedures. Because the event was specifically intended to help people to change the culture in which they worked, the trainers decided to start the process by concentrating on the subject of culture.

The learners split up into three equal groups and each group was asked to produce a definition of culture. They were also asked to make a list of some of the main features of organisational culture as they perceived it. It was explained that each of them might perceive culture differently and that they were not obliged to compromise when discussing points. The trainers explained that it was perfectly acceptable for different people to have different views.

Each group was facilitated by a trainer who took care to manage the process of discussion only and not the content itself. Otherwise there was a danger that the trainer might unduly influence the group discussion. The groups talked for about 30 minutes and then compared their findings in a plenary discussion.

The outcome enabled the trainers to identify where each of the learners stood in relation to the concepts of culture. The activity helped everyone to see the ways in which culture was perceived – the similarities and differences. The relevance of attending the event became obvious. The learners saw for themselves that if the organisation was trying to move in a particular direction and they all had these very different perceptions of where they were at that time, they would need to come together in some way for future cohesiveness. The activity produced some common ground, some common terminology and some common assumptions, values and beliefs as a basis on which to work during the week ahead.

Icebreakers and the learner's needs

Icebreakers can be used not only to break the ice but also to discover the individual needs of learners at the same time. Many trainers ask learners to explain their individual learning objectives within the overall objectives of the learning event itself. But concentrating on each individual's objectives will not help to break the ice in itself, so you need to find interesting ways to combine the two. Some suggestions are given in the remainder of this chapter.

For learners

Objectively introduced

Purpose

The purpose of this activity is to combine icebreaking with setting objectives for a learning event. It helps to identify the learning needs of individuals so that you and they can ensure that their requirements are taken into account. It also helps to give you the cultural context relating to the learners' objectives.

If this is also to be used as an icebreaker it should be explained in a reassuring and non-threatening way.

Timing

You can use this activity at the start of a learning event after the administrative and domestic details have been dealt with.

Materials

A piece of flipchart paper and a pen for each learner. Plenty of space for learners to work in pairs.

Time

Allow 20 to 30 minutes for the discussions in pairs and then 15 to 20 minutes to review and summarise.

Group size

The above timings are suitable for eight to twelve learners.

Method

- Ask learners to pair up with someone they do not know (or know the least).
- Give each learner a piece of flipchart paper and a pen.
- Ask learners to take it in turns to talk each other through the issues which they face at work and to discuss the objectives which they wish to address on the learning event as a result.
- Learners should help each other to summarise key points about their learning objectives on the flipchart and be ready to share their points with the others.

Debrief

Reassemble the group and ask each learner to present their objectives, making sure they give their name clearly and say a little about themselves by way of introduction, such as the name of their organisation or section and the job they do.

You will find that as a result of the discussion in pairs learners are likely to provide more context when they talk about each objective. This is useful in a number of ways. It will provide you with cultural background to help them achieve their detailed objectives. It will enable the rest of the group to understand why each person is attending the event. It will usually help learners to recognise how they can help each other.

It is often useful at this point to relate individual objectives to the objectives of the learning event. If particular objectives are outside the scope of the event, you can make suggestions as to how they may be fulfilled in other ways. You may wish to comment if there are any particularly unusual or exciting ways in which some of the objectives can be met. This will help to stimulate interest.

Conclusion

Adapting objective-setting in this way combines icebreaking, setting objectives and learning about the individual's culture. It provides far more depth and context than simply asking people to spend a few minutes writing down their objectives and then reading them out to the others.

Finally, in this chapter we outline two very straightforward icebreakers that also take the implications of culture into account.

Activity 3 | For learners

Pictures of objectives

This combines two of the icebreakers already described. Simply give each learner a piece of flipchart paper and a pen. Ask them to draw a picture of the things they would like to tackle or deal with during the learning event. Then, as before, ask them to display and explain their flipchart.

Because a picture is used it frees learners from some of the constraints that words can cause. Do not force them to use only pictures, however, because that may present a problem to people from some cultures. Mostly though you will find that the use of pictures brings out issues and items that many people would never have thought to mention otherwise. It often happens that deeper and more subconscious issues emerge.

Activity 4

For learners

See, feel and say

Ask the learners to write down what would happen at their workplace if they achieved their objectives by the end of the learning event. You need to ask them:

- What it would feel like.
- What they saw happening at the workplace.
- What people would be saying about it.

It may be that they cannot answer all three questions; but that in itself might indicate which mode they are most comfortable with: that is, feeling, seeing or hearing. It may also provide material for you to follow up. You could try to discover whether it is the individual who tends to use that mode or whether it is common to their culture.

Summary

In addition to helping people relax, icebreakers can help trainers to understand the cultural backgrounds of their learners.

You can use icebreakers to explore:

- The learner's general cultural context.
- The learner's perceptions.
- The learner's needs.

Many conventional icebreakers can be adapted to obtain more information on the implications of the learner's culture for the effectiveness of the learning and development process.

13 | The main event

The traditional learning event is likely to comprise a number of sessions timetabled to fit within the working day, or around mealtimes at the hotel or training centre. The sessions themselves are usually labelled according to some rational breakdown of the subject in question. The trainer's role is to make sure that each session is presented in a way that will enable learners to understand it. Such has been the format of many learning events over the years. But how can we take into account the implications of culture for the learning process?

To explore this issue we have broken down the subject of learning into three different areas, which we will cover separately. These areas are:

- Knowledge and understanding.
- Skills and abilities.
- Attitude and behaviour.

Knowledge and understanding

Knowledge and understanding sessions are usually designed to increase the level of information possessed by the learners about a particular subject. The objective is not to produce an ability to do something, merely an understanding of it. If you then want the learner to put that knowledge to use your session may have to move on to skills and abilities. A knowledge and understanding session may well be a preliminary part of a learning event.

In the case of 'total quality management', for example, the objective of the knowledge session may be for learners to understand a particular definition of quality and to understand the tools available to measure quality.

From the cultural point of view there are at least two approaches you can take. Both methods are 'right' depending on the circumstances, the desired outcome and the cultural norms.

Firstly, you can present everything to everyone, regardless of previous knowledge held by individuals. The advantages of this approach are that you ensure that everyone receives the same information and you do not have to spend time checking each individual's existing knowledge.

This approach can be particularly effective when you need to:

● Reinforce an organisational cultural message by making sure that everyone is given the information in the same way. For example, many organisations hire a large hall so they can bring their employees together and tell everyone at the same time about such issues as the organisation's performance over a certain period, the strengths and weaknesses, opportunities and threats facing the company in the future.
● Develop further learning based on a common understanding of key concepts. For example, you may want to ensure that everyone possesses the same knowledge about the organisation's approach to customer care before the skills and attitude training begins.
● Identify and recognise a problem or opportunity the organisation is facing which will require each section to develop and implement its own particular response.

Achieving such common knowledge and understanding is not so easy, though. If you have to reach large numbers of people at the same time, you may need a space as large as a sports stadium (at least one company we know of has hired one). You can run a series of events in parallel but the cultural differences of each presenter will influence the process. Briefings which cascade down through an organisation are known to be substantially affected by the cultural phenomenon of filtering. Filtering of information is often linked with people's perceived power in their culture.

The second way of developing knowledge and understanding is to provide people with only the information they require to achieve their own particular work objectives. The fundamentals of this method are:

● That people are only given the information that is relevant for them to do their own jobs.
● That different people in different parts of the organisation already have some of the knowledge required.
● That because each person or section takes a different view of the

154

issue each has different information needs.

To provide people only with information that is relevant involves a number of considerations, including:

- How will you decide what is relevant?
- What suitable delivery methods do you have for putting over knowledge on a selective basis?

Let's examine these two issues in more detail.

How will you decide what is relevant?

One way of deciding what is relevant is to ask the learners for their perceptions. Sometimes a briefing document that sets out key areas to be discussed will help learners to decide what is relevant.

Another approach is to seek the views of the learners' managers. The managers may well have a better overview of the whole situation, and may be aware of changes affecting the work. Most of us realise that we do not always recognise our own faults and failings and there are also occasions when we are unaware of our need to know about a certain topic.

The 'best' approach to deciding what is relevant will depend on a combination of factors, including:

- Time.
- People's availability.
- How much people are prepared to reveal.
- To what extent 'the manager knows best'.
- To what extent the subordinate can be involved in the process.

Of course, the answers to these questions depend not just on the facts, but also on cultural norms.

What delivery methods do you use?

Here are some examples of how culture can affect your choice. If, for instance, the workforce is 'empowered', then self-managed learning may be appropriate and positively welcomed. Where training is seen as a remedial tool, then more directive methods tend to be employed.

Many trainers find it more difficult to organise and manage a process where knowledge is developed on a selective basis. They find it can often take longer to achieve even though the total quantity of what you are delivering is less. Whether it will cost more will depend on the time saved by individuals not attending an event unnecessarily and the time involved in individualising a programme.

We have given some ideas as to how knowledge needs can be met. It is likely that not all the ideas fit your personal or organisational cultural values and norms. The most important step is probably for you to assess the methods you could use to meet learning needs in the areas of knowledge and understanding. Explore methods that are appropriate for the culture of your organisation for:

- Ensuring that all learners receive the same message.
- Enabling learners to receive just the information that is relevant to them.

Also think about how you would discover if the learning had taken place successfully. That will form the basis of your evaluation.

Skills and abilities

Skills and abilities learning may involve some knowledge and understanding but goes much further because the objective is to enable the learners to do something new or differently. The limitations of such learning are that while the learners frequently learn the skills they do not learn them in the environment in which they are to be used. Much management training and development takes place in this way.

There are two main ways to help forge the vital link between the application of skills and the appropriate environment. First you can attempt to understand the learner's culture, work and organisation so fully that you are in a position to suggest how to make the transfer of learning, to provide the right solutions and methods. Occasionally a trainer who has spent considerable time working with a particular section will be in a position to do this. But, over time the section the trainer understood so well will change. The norms and values may also change. And what if the learners are from many different sections or companies?

The second way to forge a link is to enable the learners to make the transfer of learning themselves, to choose the answers and solutions that they believe will work. By following the approach suggested in this book, so that you have some idea of the assumptions, values and beliefs which the learners subscribe to, you can help the learners to be more aware of the culture in which they work and thus be in a better position to find solutions.

Whether you help learners to relate the skills they have developed to the culture in which they work before or after they have had some skills practice will depend on how relevant they believe the skills are to the issues they have to deal with. It is probably necessary to wait until they recognise and understand the skills in question from a knowledge point of view before attempting to relate them to culture.

You can make the link with culture by asking the learners to consider, either individually or as a group (depending on which is more suitable for their learning style), each of the skills to which they have been introduced. They should concentrate particularly on skills which are new to them and on skills which they would not have considered using in the past to help with an issue. Ask them to list the parts of the environment (the culture) that could support the use of those skills, and the parts of the environment that would hinder the use of those skills. The learners can then use this information to help them decide how to apply the skills they have developed.

Take negotiation skills as an example. Your learners may work in an organisational culture that supports skills which build a Win/Win relationship with customers. The skill of negotiating in a hard way therefore, that demonstrates that a learner is a tough, no-nonsense negotiator who sets out to win with little regard for whether the other party achieves a win, is unlikely to fit a Win/Win culture. So the main part of your learning event can concentrate either on helping the learners to fit the prevailing culture or on changing the culture to fit the style of the learners. This links up with questions of attitude and behaviour which we will explore next.

Attitude and behaviour

The type of learning that involves changes in attitude is probably the most difficult to achieve, but it is the one most directly related to culture. Attitudinal changes are not so much about developing knowledge and skill, although those can be important elements, it is more concerned with helping learners to change the way in which they think about and approach issues. It involves changing assumptions, values and beliefs.

The most common way of approaching this type of learning is to centre on managing change. It could be argued that all learning involves change as learners adapt to new knowledge, new skills or new attitudes. However, there is a significant difference when learning involves a change in culture. Not only may learners have to adapt to new knowledge and skills, they have to cope with a change in assumptions, values and beliefs as well.

Hence, during the main part of a learning event which is dealing with a change in culture, learners may feel uncomfortable and threatened as they experience a challenge to the deep-rooted beliefs and values they hold and which may have served them well during their work-

157

ing life. During this main part of a learning event you, as the trainer, can either work with a learner's culture and help them to adapt to new ways of thinking, or you can ignore their culture and risk what to them may appear to be a confrontational challenge. Learners may not even be aware of what is happening but if they perceive confrontation to be taking place their reaction may be one of:

- **Disagreement with ideas and suggestions**
  This reaction may be expressed through silence, withdrawal, reluctance to take part in an activity or discussion, or by using ridicule or humour to back up their beliefs, putting forward opposing points of view or being aggressive. These reactions are known as 'fight, flight, freeze' behaviours and are quite common responses from learners who feel pressured into doing something which they cannot handle within their existing cultural frameworks.
- **Reluctance to use the learning**
  During the main part of the learning event, learners may well join in with what is happening and may even find that they can relate to it quite strongly. The problems occur if the learner realises that the ideas do not suit the culture in which they work and believes that the ideas or skills cannot be used in their workplace. This can lead to a sharp deterioration in the main part of a learning event and, unless the trainer understands the link with culture, can be quite mystifying.

Activities

During the main part of the learning event it is possible that you may want to use interactive learning activities to help learners. You will probably have a range of activities which you are used to running and with which you feel comfortable. However, you might not have thought about the activities in terms of culture. So to continue our theme of taking the implications of culture on learning and development into account, we show in the next activity how a conventional learning activity can be adapted to work with learners' cultures.

Activity 5 | For learners

What makes a good manager?

Purpose

This activity involves learners listing the qualities of a good manager but in a way that explores their cultures. It studies the influence of learners' cultures on what makes a 'good manager'.

For example, the objective might be:

> At the end of the session learners will be able to identify a range of management styles and describe situations in which each might be most appropriate.

Group size

Up to 12 learners.

Method

The key points relating to how you would run this activity in context with the whole session are:

- Explain the session objective(s).
- Ask learners to make individual lists of the qualities of a good manager. Allow five to ten minutes for this.
- Ask learners to share their lists briefly. Allow ten minutes.
- In groups of no more than four, ask learners to discuss what they mean by a 'manager', what they mean by 'good' and what they mean by 'qualities'. (This will help to identify some of the cultural differences.) Groups should record key points on a flipchart, including minority views. Allow 30 minutes for the discussion.
- Groups share key points. Encourage individuals to give examples to support their comments.

Additional information

By now you should have considerable information about the values, assumptions, beliefs and mindsets influencing the learners' perceptions of 'what makes a good manager'. You may wish to summarise the cultural differences and similarities with the group.

You now have a number of choices. Let's assume that your objective was to cover some key management styles, such as 'the manager tells them what to do' through to 'the manager sets the boundaries and leaves them to decide', to ensure that they know when each key concept might be particularly suitable. You could:

- Give the theory, or a framework for examining management styles, and ask them to relate it to their environment using the preparatory work on 'what makes a good manager'. This may be appropriate if the learners have already described a wide range of management styles and can identify with them. It may be that they just need a framework for categorising the separate pieces of information they have on management styles. Or:
- Use the examples and situations the learners have already described and help them to generalise and conceptualise. Help them to relate examples to theory, for instance. Use the knowledge you have gained about their cultures to decide which areas can be covered quickly, because they can identify with them, and which areas will need more careful handling because the concepts are alien to their culture. Or:
- Guide the learners through a series of practical exercises. Each person should take turns in 'managing' so that the styles demonstrated can be discussed. This may be important if the cultural differences are so strong that they have difficulty in relating to the ideas described by each other during discussion.

In each case though, you will be able to relate to the learners' culture and their perceptions of 'what makes a good manager'. You will be able to see 'where they are coming from' and use their examples and ideas wherever possible. You will be better able to help them explore new areas because you will have a better picture of the limitations and constraints created by their cultural beliefs.

Summary

When deciding how to design and deliver the main part of a learning event you will need to consider a variety of factors, including culture.

This is important whether you are working with knowledge and understanding, skills and abilities or attitude and behaviour.

Knowledge

Presenting everything to everyone in the same way can help to:

- Reinforce an organisational message.
- Ensure that everyone has the same information.
- Prevent filtering of information which is often linked with perceived power in a culture.

Presenting only the knowledge that people need or want takes account of:

- Different levels of existing knowledge.
- Different views.
- Different cultural needs.

Skills and abilities

You can attempt to understand the learners' cultures so that you can suggest how they may use their skills and abilities at work.

You can help the learners to be more aware of their own cultures so that they can suggest how they can use their skills and abilities at work.

Attitude and behaviour

Attitudinal changes often involve helping learners to change the way in which they think about concepts, how situations are approached and their assumptions, values and beliefs in relation to issues.

Adapting learning activities

It is often possible to adapt activities which you already use so that you work with learners' cultures rather than in ignorance of the implications of their cultures.

14 | Breaking the rules

The material you provide for a learning event may support and strengthen the existing culture, or it may be designed to introduce new ways of working – ways that are different from those supported by the current culture. The material you provide may well be 'best practice' but how does it fit in with the prevailing culture?

Examine carefully the material you are providing. If it supports the existing culture, ask yourself the following questions:

- Am I taking the easy way out, giving them what they want to hear, rather than what is needed?
- Am I reinforcing the existing culture when senior management is trying to take the organisation in a different direction?
- Does the material conform to existing culture because it makes me feel comfortable?
- Am I reinforcing existing culture because it is the most appropriate one for the needs of the organisation in the short- to medium-term?

If the material you provide does not conform to the existing culture ask yourself these questions:

- Is the material different because my culture (or the culture of my section) is different from the culture of the main organisation or from the learner's culture?
- How successful can my material be if the support for the ideas is not present because they are contrary to the prevailing culture?
- Will flouting convention cause disapproval in other parts of the organisation: for example, with learners' bosses, those who may

influence your promotion, those who release budgets? Will the disapproval be beneficial to the organisation – in the short-term and in the long-term?

- Will nonconformity help to revive the organisation? Will it inspire new ways of working and so help to change the culture to suit the organisation's current and future needs?
- Will breaking the rules help to win respect and credibility so that I can better facilitate the learning process?
- Will breaking the rules be seen as inciting rebellion and upsetting the status quo which has been acceptable for the last few years?
- Will providing material which is contrary to the existing culture be a waste of time when it comes to the transfer of learning back to work?

Learning and development often involves 'doing something new'. The something new may be within the existing cultural framework or outside it. If you are working outside the existing framework you are likely to experience such situations as:

- Learners' managers not supporting the ideas and techniques from the learning event.
- Learners feeling that the methods are not relevant or workable in their jobs.

If you are working outside the existing cultural framework you may find that it helps to:

- Win approval from influential people within your organisation.
- Try the ideas out with people who are not so firmly entrenched in the prevailing culture and who are amenable to change. Let them champion the ideas after the learning event for you.
- Explain why change is needed. Involve learners in the need for change. Encourage people from senior management to express their commitment to the ideas and become involved.
- Help learners to work out how they can modify and adapt the ideas. Help them to work out ways of implementation to take account of existing culture.

A useful exercise is to complete a training audit to see how compatible you tend to be with the learner's culture or the organisation's culture, or whether you tend to 'break the rules'. Details of how to conduct an audit are provided in Activity 15 on page167.

The example that follows is of a training audit completed by a trainer involved with supervisory and management development.

Training topic	How it fits in with the existing organisational culture
1) Helping deputy first line managers to develop training skills for on the job training of their staff	Fits in with existing culture. The organisation feels that a lot of technical and day to day personal training should be done by these deputy first line managers rather than by trainers external to the section. The culture is supportive of directly job related training done in a practical way. This is helping to strengthen training taking place on a regular basis.
2) Appraisal training	Does not fit with existing culture. The current culture is one of telling staff once a year how they've been doing. The current training approach puts forward that appraisal should be regular two way discussions about evaluating and learning from past performance, planning future performance, and planning any training or other resources that may be needed to enable that performance. This is causing frustration because senior management say they wish appraisal to take place in this way (but don't practise it themselves). Many managers want to use appraisal in the way they have been trained, but the culture of the organisation is not supportive in reality.

Table 1. Training topic: How it fits with the existing organisational culture

For trainers

Content and method audit

Purpose

The purpose of this activity is to help you to determine if the content and methods you tend to use support the existing culture or are contrary to it in some way.

Method

From the point of view of the cultural values, assumptions and beliefs on which they are based, conduct an audit of:

- The content of the learning and development events with which you are involved.
- The methods and style used.

See page 165 if you want to refer to a worked example.

Depending on whether you are more interested in a trend or in a detailed analysis, either write a summary of all the learning events with which you are involved or cover one or two in detail.

Write down:

- The topic, course title or learning event title.
- A brief description of what it is about, in two or three sentences at the most.
- The ways you feel it conforms to or supports the learner's or organisation's existing culture.
- The ways you feel it is contrary to the learner's or organisation's culture.

Debrief

- How does the content and methods fit in with the prevailing culture?

- Does it strengthen existing culture or is it outside the existing framework?

Conclusion

In each case it is worth considering the implications. Evaluate carefully whether you are:

- Strengthening an existing culture when you should be helping it to change.
- Creating extra pressure by challenging the existing culture unnecessarily.

Summary

Breaking the rules can have a positive or negative effective depending on the circumstances.

Does the material and style of your training tend to support the existing culture or is it contrary to it?

What is the rationale behind your answer?

- Are your reasons valid and helpful?
- Or does your rationale help you to take the easy way out without necessarily helping the learning and development process?

15 | Debriefing, feedback and review

Many trainers conduct feedback and review sessions with a very limited range of tools. The tools they do use are often ones they feel comfortable with and not necessarily ones which learners can identify with. This is probably an appropriate time to reassess the feedback and review methods which you tend to use. To what extent are they an extension of the culture to which you subscribe? How alien are they to your learners?

It is very dangerous to try to force people from another culture to accept your perceptions as the *only* correct perceptions. Selling your ideas as superior to their ideas invites rebellion, resistance, withdrawal and criticism. It can lead to the perception that you are not 'in the real world'.

Remember that your perceptions of what is appropriate or inappropriate, helpful or unhelpful are based on your own experiences, assumptions, values and beliefs – your culture. Behaviour which is considered acceptable in one culture may be very unacceptable in another.

Culture influences what people consider to be new, different, helpful, acceptable, obvious, strange. To help them to explore new ideas you need to recognise what learners see as important and relevant.

It may be easy for you to see how to implement an idea based on your cultural experiences but it may not be so easy for learners to implement the same idea in the environment in which they work. They may need to adapt the idea to suit the culture in which they operate. They may need to use an entirely different approach. By recognising and acknowledging differences you are more likely to win their trust and so be in a better position to help them to take steps forward in their development.

The language which you and the learners use in the feedback and review sessions is important too. How you phrase your message can influence whether it is acceptable or not. Given below are two different methods of reviewing a role play where the learner taking the role of interviewer is having difficulty in drawing out information from an interviewee.

The direct approach

Learners in some cultures would appreciate a direct approach to the review. You could ask, for example:

- How could you have tackled that in a different way which might have produced more information from the interviewee?

In this way you are addressing the interviewer directly and referring to the way in which they conducted the role play. You are directly asking for their ideas.

A more general approach

With people of another culture you might need to say:

- If a situation of that sort arose at work what are some of the options one could choose from?

Here you are de-personalising the situation and reviewing in a more general way. You are not commenting on what the individual in the role play actually did.

The trainer needs a range of ways of dealing with feedback and review sessions so that the different needs of different cultures can be taken into account.

Activity 16	**For trainers**

Evaluating feedback sessions

Purpose

This is an activity for a group of trainers who are involved in facilitating feedback sessions. It is particularly relevant to those involved with softer skills, such as management and interpersonal skills development.

Method

Work in groups of three or four and concentrate on situations in which you have facilitated feedback to learners from a different culture (this could be because they worked for a different organisation, different department, and so on).

- Take it in turns for each person to share a successful case and a disappointing or unhelpful case.
- For each case try as a group to identify the cultural values and beliefs that influenced the outcome.

Some questions to help you in the analysis would be:

- What were the differences and similarities in cultural values between the learner and the trainer?
- In what ways did these differences and similarities help or hinder the learning process?
- To what extent was the trainer (and maybe the learner) aware of the differences at the time?
- What was done to manage any differences in perception?
- What was done to gain new perspectives?

Look especially for differences, similarities, trends or patterns.

Debrief

Help each other to plan how to capitalise on the successes and how to tackle the areas you are not so satisfied with. Recognise that culture is only one of many reasons why a debrief or review may not have gone as successfully as you would have liked, but it is an important one that is currently often overlooked.

Conclusion

Cultural assumptions, values and beliefs are often unconscious. They can help or hinder the feedback and review process. It is worth exploring further the similarities, differences, trends and patterns of values, assumptions and beliefs which influence effective feedback and review sessions.

Summary

Your perceptions of what is right, wrong, appropriate and inappropriate are based on your own assumptions, values and beliefs which your learners may not share.

As a result you may find it more effective to adapt your methods of feedback to link up with the learner's culture.

The style, method and language which you use all need to be considered carefully.

Review your feedback sessions to identify the extent to which you all spoke the same language from the same point of view.

Part IV — The way forward

16 | The cultural dimension

We all recognise that people from different cultures have different ways of doing things – from eating and family behaviour to beliefs, rituals and language. But many of us are only just beginning to recognise and appreciate the different cultural frameworks that influence working life: the way we organise, manage, lead, motivate and control. A culture which has a high incidence of uncertainty avoidance will manage situations very differently from one which has a low incidence. Cultures evaluate time in very different ways and short-term planning may be a matter of days for one culture and months for another in regard to the same project.

For trainers to work effectively across cultures is a challenging and sensitive task. For their design and delivery many trainers use Western researched models, especially ones which originate in the United States. Many of these models are based on:

● Being pro-active.
● Encouraging individual contribution.
● Developing people on an individual basis.
● 'Humanistic' values concerned with integrating personal and organisational goals.
● Decision making involving trust.
● Equalising power.

However, bear in mind that organisational cultures are often based on very different assumptions and rationales. Those assumptions and rationales have validity in those cultures.

Trainers are in a unique position to learn to listen to individuals from different cultures. They have the opportunity to respond to them with sensitivity and awareness, to negotiate and manage the differences in a positive and beneficial way, and to accommodate differences in a way that will facilitate the learning process.

With training and practice we can learn to recognise different cultural frameworks and the assumptions, values and beliefs on which they are based. By doing so we will be in a much better position to facilitate the learning process.

When it comes to communicating effectively across cultures there are some factors that will have become clear from working through this book.

- The same words mean different things to different people and cultural context is one of the many factors influencing their perception.
- We hear, see and feel things which were not communicated, and often not intended.
- We do not hear, see or feel things which were communicated. We sift, sort, miss and misinterpret many of the communications around us. Our culture is one of a number of important factors which influence how this is done.
- We each perceive the same things in different ways.

If people have never had to consider a different culture they tend to assume that their way of doing things is the right way. People who have worked in one section or one branch of an organisation all their working life are likely to be entrenched in the values and beliefs they hold about that area. That is quite natural and to be expected. Wider experience can help but is not necessarily the answer if they continue to carry those values with them and impose them on their new companions.

Trainers often have to manage learning events that involve a wide diversity of cultures, not necessarily in terms of national or ethnic cultures but in terms of functional, organisational and geographical cultures. We need to recognise that these latter cultural frameworks are just as powerful and relevant to the learning process. Success in the future will lie in a trainer's ability to bridge and manage those cultural differences and to use them to facilitate the learning process.

The distortion caused by different cultural frameworks is an issue from which trainers cannot hide. It is one that can and has to be addressed if learners are to be helped to make progress.

17 | The transfer of learning

Throughout this book we have tried to provide you with ideas and help on taking the implications of culture for the learning and development process into account. You will have been able to use activities to identify cultural differences in different learners. You will also have had the opportunity to understand a little about the cultural biases that you will be bringing to the learning and development process as a trainer. However, the final aspect of the process – helping learners to transfer their learning to the workplace – rests not only on the work that you do, but on the attitude of the learner's organisation.

To explain this concept we need to examine the various philosophies which organisations have adopted towards learning and development and to recognise the possible implications for learning transfer. They can be grouped under the following headings:

- Organisations with no learning philosophy.
- Organisations with a people philosophy.
- Organisations with a process philosophy.
- Organisations with a people/process philosophy.
- Organisations with a cultural philosophy.

Organisations with no learning philosophy

In organisations without a learning philosophy training often happens in a haphazard way. There is usually little coordination of learning and development with any type of business plan – if indeed such a plan exists. Much of the training is achieved by sending learners to external public courses. Neither courses nor internal training are linked to any

181

career development or succession planning processes. The internal training department will tend to run the courses the trainers are good at running and whether they are beneficial to the learners or the business will be more a matter of good luck than philosophy.

The positive side of this kind of situation is that the trainers are usually very dedicated and committed to producing high quality courses, despite the fact that the organisation may be unwilling to make learning and development an integral part of the strategic business plan. In this kind of organisation training is seen as something that the training department 'does to people' and has responsibility for. The idea that the responsibility for learning rests with the learners is not normally recognised. Nor is the word 'learning'.

As a trainer you will easily be able to recognise the signs of this kind of company. You will find yourself running the same learning events each year. If there is a financial squeeze then your department will be one of the first to feel it. Training, learning and personal development are thought of as secondary to the 'real work'. How often do you come across managers who don't have time to attend the time management course for instance?

It is not difficult to see why this philosophy – or rather lack of philosophy – will cause difficulty with transfer of learning back to the workplace. Any new ideas or techniques may well threaten the status quo.

Organisations with a people philosophy

Many organisations adopt a culture which centres on the people working for them. The basic philosophy within this type of organisation is to look after the employees first and foremost. The methodology used to develop the organisation and move it forward through change also concentrates on people. Time and resources are spent on developing individuals with the expectation that they will naturally change systems and processes where necessary in order to manage the organisation effectively. Most learning is handled by the training department and learning events are held at a properly resourced training centre or hotel so that the learners are comfortable and well looked after.

The usual outcome is that the learners find the learning and development fairly straightforward to assimilate but once back in the workplace they find the same old pressures and standards still in place, so their behaviour quickly reverts. The learning will tend to be at a 'knowledge or skill' level and the 'old' ways, still prevailing within the workplace, will serve to reinforce the traditional practices making life too comfortable to change the status quo.

If you take a people approach to learning and development you are likely to be concerned with issues such as:

- Working relationships.
- Mentoring and coaching.
- Interpersonal skills.
- Constructive feedback.
- Self-development.
- Continuous development.

Organisations with a process philosophy

Organisations with a process philosophy are at the other end of the scale to organisations with a people philosophy. They will favour 'management by controlling what people do'. There will be checkpoints built into most processes so that the work can be checked by a second person. Change will be handled by writing new procedures (usually created outside the department or company), designing new systems and putting new processes into place.

The theory behind this philosophy is that people will adapt to the demands of the new processes and change. The reality is that, although they may well be learning new skills to meet the new processes, when they return to their work they will tend to bend the new ways to serve the old. The previous methods will still exist – despite being formally removed – because the basic organisational philosophy will still be the same. The workforce will merely be acting out a new set of rules.

Many organisations see this philosophy as one that provides successful change – but change of what? Certainly there may be new rules and procedures in place but the way the workforce approaches problem solving will still be the same.

For example, one company we know of introduced a Total Quality Management (TQM) system into the organisation. An enormous amount of money was spent in buying in the new process, which was installed as an 'off the shelf' process. Each employee was given a set training course on problem identification and problem solving skills.

Once the process was in place it was enforced with a rigid set of rules which were designed to ensure that the taught skills were applied. The policing was such that those found not to be following the rules (even though still achieving organisational objectives and, in many cases, evolving better processes for following the TQM philosophy) were required to provide justification for their actions and then to move back in line. The senior managers, who were thought of as the 'owners' of the process by the workforce, were seen to 'talk a good game' but not perceived to follow their own rigid set of rules.

183 The outcome was expensive and fairly disastrous. The TQM approach reinforced what had already been a militaristic style of management, with rank playing a large part in the use of authority. Subsequent attempts within the organisation to introduce more participative approaches to managing were met with resistance from the senior managers and scepticism from the rest of the workforce. So the 'change' resulted in a reinforcement of the status quo. Many years of battling against entrenched values and beliefs would be required to achieve real change.

If you take a process approach to learning and development you are likely to begin by concentrating on:

- Objectives.
- Planning and forecasting.
- Monitoring and control.
- Developing procedures.
- Evaluation.
- Setting and maintaining standards and quality.

At this point it would be worth summarising what we have discussed so far. The people philosophy seeks to achieve change through people. If people can be taught new skills and provided with new information then they will return to the workplace and initiate the changes required. That sounds very logical but it often doesn't work. The process philosophy seeks to achieve change through new work methods and practices which are enforced with rules and checkpoints. If systems and procedures can be changed then people will adapt to them and adopt new skills and approaches. This also sounds logical, but often it doesn't work either.

What about those organisations that combine the two – the people and the process philosophies?

Organisations with a people/process philosophy

The people philosophy and the process philosophy are not mutually exclusive. Some organisations have used both in their approach to learning and development. This means that as well as enabling their people to learn new skills to cope with a new environment (such as alternative management techniques) they have also developed new methods and systems to support the direction the business is taking and trained the workforce to use these new ways (process training). The results have been impressive. Some of these organisations have shown clearly measurable changes in employee behaviour and some have been able to maintain these changes with seemingly little effort. Some others, however, have found that behaviour changes have only lasted in the short-term. The question raised is why should employees of some organisations be able to maintain behavioural changes while employees of other organisations revert to traditional ways and attitudes?

Our conclusions are that for learning and development to take place within an organisation and to be maintained attention has to be paid to more than people and processes. The success of these two approaches rests on a very powerful third factor – culture.

Organisations with a cultural philosophy

For learning and development to be effective it is not enough to take a people approach and it is not enough to take a process approach. Processes won't work without people who are suitably skilled and knowledgeable to work them. Even if the emphasis is on both people and processes it is still not enough because people and processes don't operate in a vacuum – they operate in a culture (or across a number of cultures) in an organisation. So unless the implications of culture are taken into account learning and development can be ineffective because they are working out of context – out of cultural context.

If you take a cultural approach you are likely to consider the following:

- Personal and organisational assumptions and beliefs.
- Myths and mindsets.
- Norms and values.

In other words you will be examining the culture in which the people and the processes operate.

Diagram 11 shows the link between the three dimensions: people, processes and culture. The learning and development process can start at any point on the triangle, and may revisit any point a number of times. This book gives you the methods and ideas to tackle the culture dimension of this model.

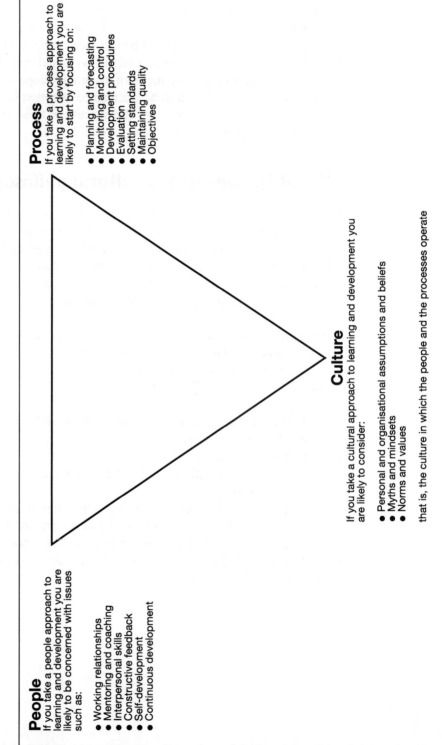

Process

If you take a process approach to learning and development you are likely to start by focusing on:

- Planning and forecasting
- Monitoring and control
- Development procedures
- Evaluation
- Setting standards
- Maintaining quality
- Objectives

Culture

If you take a cultural approach to learning and development you are likely to consider:

- Personal and organisational assumptions and beliefs
- Myths and mindsets
- Norms and values

that is, the culture in which the people and the processes operate

People

If you take a people approach to learning and development you are likely to be concerned with issues such as:

- Working relationships
- Mentoring and coaching
- Interpersonal skills
- Constructive feedback
- Self-development
- Continuous development

186 | **Diagram 11.** The three dimensions of the learning and development process

18 | Into action

We said at the beginning of this book that there are many factors which influence an effective learning event and one very neglected one is culture.

We identified a number of questions which you may well be facing at the moment. Let's examine them again:

Trainer
Q   How can I be more effective in the way I help people with the learning and development process?

Senior mangement
Q   How can we get better return on investment on learning and development?

Learner
Q   How can I get help and ideas I can use back at work?
Q   Will the learning event meet my needs?

Learner's manager
Q   Will the learning event make a difference to the learner when they return to work?

By now you will be better able to respond to these differing demands on you as a trainer by:

- Identifying your own cultural biases and allowing for them.
- Being aware of the implications of taking others down the path of your own values and beliefs.
- Recognising the assumptions, values and beliefs held by each learner.
- Tailoring learning events, where appropriate, to take account of each learner's different assumptions, values and beliefs.

- Being aware that each organisation consists of many cultures, some of which are extremely complex.
- Recognising and taking these cultures into account so that learners can be helped more effectively with the transfer of learning back to work.

Use the Appendix 'The implications of culture – an action checklist' to help plan your way forward.

The implications of culture – an action checklist

Use the following headings to help take stock of how you are going to manage the implications of culture on the learning and development process. For each item consider:

- Whether you are satisfied with how you tackle the issue.
- What changes, if any, you would like to make in your approach.
- Key issues which you feel are important to follow up.

- How people are selected for a learning event.

- Choice of training team, trainer's role.

- Skills of the trainer(s).

- Knowledge of learners before the event.

- Transfer of learning.

- Advertising literature.

- Application form.

- Briefing notes.

- Joining instructions.

- Pre-course work.

- Pre-course questionnaires.

- Icebreakers.

- Main part activities.

- Debriefing, feedback and review.

Reproduced from *Dealing with Difference*
by Teresa Williams and Adrian Green, Gower, Aldershot, 1994.

Sources and resources

The following items are referred to in the main text of the book.

Armstrong, Michael. (1989), *Personnel and the Bottom Line*, London: IPM.
Armstrong looks specifically at corporate culture and provides definitions and descriptions of what corporate culture encompasses.

Hofstede, Geert. (1984), *Culture's Consequences*, Newbury Park, USA: Sage.
Describes Hofstede's research in considerable detail.

Schein, Edgar. (1984), 'Suppose we took culture seriously', *Academy of Management OD Newsletter*, Summer.
Contains a fairly detailed definition of culture.

Young, Arthur. (1986), *The Manager's Handbook, The Practical Guide to Successful Management*, London: Marshall.
Contains useful definitions of terms related to company culture.

The following have helped us in developing the material in this book – you may find them useful too.

The Eye of the Storm (30 minutes)
This film shows an experiment by Jane Elliot which enabled children to learn from the effects of discrimination. They experienced how different cultural values may influence the learning process.

A Class Divided (60 minutes)
A follow-up of the people shown in *The Eye of the Storm* some 15 years later. It repeats the same experiment with prison staff.

These are powerful training films which illustrate how cultural differences can develop into prejudices. Copyright of Yale University. Available from a number of suppliers including Concord Video and Film Council, Ipswich, Suffolk, UK (Phone 0473 726012).

de Bono, Edward. (1990), *I am right – you are wrong,* London: Penguin.
A useful book for developing an understanding of perception based on more fluid patterns of thinking.

Byham, William C. *Zapp, The Lightning of Empowerment,*
London: Century.
Explains how you can help to develop a culture of empowerment.

Hoff, Benjamin. (1982), *The Tao of Pooh*, London: Methuen.
A good example of how to avoid stereotyping and making assumptions. An unconventional approach but great fun.

Hofstede, Geert. (1991), *Cultures and Organizations – Software of the mind. Intercultural Cooperation and its Importance for Survival,* Maidenhead, UK: McGraw-Hill.
This book draws on the conclusions of Hofstede's earlier work, *Culture's Consequences*. Its objective 'is to help in dealing with the differences in thinking, feeling, and acting of people around the globe'. Chapter 10 usefully summarises his views on surviving in a multicultural world.

Honey, Peter, and Mumford, Alan. (1992), *The Manual of Learning Styles*, Maidenhead, UK: Peter Honey.
Describes how people have different learning styles. Includes a questionnaire for identifying four different styles.

Building a Better Team
A handbook for
managers and facilitators

Peter Moxon

Team leadership and team development are central to the modern manager's ability to "achieve results through other people". Successful team building requires knowledge and skill, and the aim of this handbook is to provide both. Using a unique blend of concepts, practical guidance and exercises, the author explains both the why and the how of team development.

Drawing on his extensive experience as manager and consultant, Peter Moxon describes how groups develop, how trust and openness can be encouraged, and the likely problems overcome. As well as detailed advice on the planning and running of teambuilding programmes the book contains a series of activities, each one including all necessary instructions and support material.

Irrespective of the size or type of organization involved, Building a Better Team offers a practical, comprehensive guide to managers, facilitators and team leaders seeking improved performance.

Contents

1993   208 pages   0 566 07424 9

Gower

Empowering People at Work

Nancy Foy

This is a book written, says the author, "for the benefit of practical managers coping with real people in real organizations". Part I shows how the elements of empowerment work together: performance focus, teams, leadership and face-to-face communication. Part II explains how to manage the process of empowerment, even in a climate of "downsizing" and "delayering". It includes chapters on networking, listening, running effective team meetings, giving feedback, training and using employee surveys. Part III contains case studies of IBM and British Telecom and examines the way they have developed employee communication to help achieve corporate objectives.

The final section comprises a review of communication channels that can be used to enhance the empowerment process, an extensive set of survey questions to be selected on a "pick and mix" basis and an annotated guide to further reading.

Empowerment is probably the most important concept in the world of management today, and Nancy Foy's new book will go a long way towards helping managers to "make it happen".

Contents

March 1994   200 pages   0 566 07436 2

Gower

Evaluating Management Development, Training and Education
Second Edition

Mark Easterby-Smith

This ambitious book offers a comprehensive guide to evaluation as applied to management development. It deals in detail with the technical aspects of evaluation, but its main value probably lies in its treatment of more subtle and possibly more important questions such as the politics of using evaluations, the range of purposes to which they may be put, and the effect of different contexts on evaluation practice.

The new edition reflects the many changes that have taken place in the world of management since the original text was compiled, in particular the Management Charter Initiative and the move towards competence-based training. The text has been updated throughout, and many new examples and case studies have been added, including a number from Europe and North America.

For anyone concerned with management development, whether as teacher, trainer or consultant, Dr Easterby-Smith's text will be indispensable.

Contents

1993   216 pages   0 566 07307 2

Gower

A Handbook for Training Strategy

Martyn Sloman

The traditional approach to training in the organization is no longer effective. That is the central theme of Martyn Sloman's challenging book. A new model is required that will reflect the complexity of organizational life, changes in the HRD function and the need to involve line management. This Handbook introduces such a model and describes the practical implications not only for human resource professionals and training managers but also for line managers.

Martyn Sloman writes as an experienced training manager and his book is concerned above all with implementation. Thus his text is supported by numerous questionnaires, survey instruments and specimen documents. It also contains the findings of an illuminating survey of best training practice carried out among UK National Training Award winners.

The book is destined to make a significant impact on the current debate about how to improve organizational performance. With its thought-provoking argument and practical guidance it will be welcomed by everyone with an interest in the business of training and development.

Contents

April 1994   200 pages   0 566 07393 5

Gower

Handbook of Management Games
Fifth Edition
Chris Elgood

What kinds of management game are now available? How do they differ from one another? How do they compare with other ways of learning? Where can I find the most suitable games for the objectives I have in mind? Handbook of Management Games offers detailed answers to these questions and many others. For this fifth edition the text has been virtually rewritten to take account of new developments. The result is a comprehensive and up-to-date guide to choosing and using games for management training and development.

Part One of the Handbook examines the characteristics and applications of the different types of game. It explains the methods by which they promote learning and the situations for which they are best suited.

Part Two comprises a directory of some 300 management games, compiled from questionnaires completed by their producers. Each game is described in terms of its target group, subject areas, nature and purpose, and the means by which the outcome is established and made known. The entries also give administrative details such as the number of players, the number of teams and the time required. A specially designed system of indexes enables readers to locate precisely those games that would be suitable for their own situation.

In its new edition Chris Elgood's Handbook remains an indispensable work for anyone concerned with management development.

1993   352 pages   0 566 07306 4

Gower

How Managers Can Develop Managers

Alan Mumford

Managers are constantly being told that they are responsible for developing other managers. This challenging book explains why and how this should be done.

Moving beyond the familiar territory of appraisal, coaching and courses, Professor Mumford examines ways of using day-to-day contact to develop managers. The emphasis is on learning from experience - from the job itself, from problems and opportunities, from bosses, mentors and colleagues.

Among the topics covered are:
- recognizing learning opportunities
- understanding the learning process
- what being helped involves
- the skills required to develop others
- the idea of reciprocity ("I help you, you help me")

Throughout the text there are exercises designed to connect the reader's own experience to the author's ideas. The result is a powerful and innovative work from one of Europe's foremost writers on management development.

Contents

1993   240 pages   0 566 07403 6

Gower

A Manual for Change

Terry Wilson

Change is now the only constant, as the cliché has it, and organizations who fail to master change are likely to find themselves undone by it.

In this unique manual, Terry Wilson provides the tools for planning and implementing a systematic organizational change programme. The first section enables the user to determine the scope and scale of the programme. Next, a change profile is completed based on twelve key factors. Finally, each of the factors is reviewed in the context of the user's own organization. Questionnaries and exercises are provided throughout and any manager working through these will have not only a clear understanding of the change process but also specific plans ready to put into action.

Derived from the author's experience of working with organizations at every level and in a wide range of industries, the manual will be invaluable to directors, managers, consultants and professional trainers battling to help their organizations survive and flourish in an increasingly turbulent environment.

Contents

Using this manual • Change programme focus: The scale of change • Change process profile: The twelve factors • Factor one Perspectives: Maintaining the overall view • Factor two The change champion: Leading the change • Factor three The nature of change: Identifying the change affecting us • Factor four Unified management vision: Importance of management agreement • Factor five Change of organizational philosophy: Modernizing the organization • Factor six Change phases: Four phases of change • Factor seven The 10/90 rule: Vision and real change • Factor eight Transitional management: Management role and style • Factor nine Teamwork: Importance of teams • Factor ten Changing behaviour: Identifying the critical factors • Factor eleven Expertise and resources: Assessing requirements • Factor twelve Dangers and pitfalls: Planning to avoid difficulties.

March 1994   230 pages   0 566 07460 5

Gower

Problem Solving
in Groups
Second Edition
Mike Robson

Modern scientific research has demonstrated that groups are likely to solve problems more effectively than individuals. As most of us knew already, two heads (or more) are better than one. In organizations it makes sense to harness the power of the group both to deal with problems already identified and to generate ideas for enhancing effectiveness by reducing costs, increasing productivity and the like.

In this revised and updated edition of his successful book, Mike Robson first introduces the concepts and methods involved. Then, after setting out the advantages of the group approach, he examines in detail each of the eight key problem solving techniques. The final part of the book explains how to present proposed solutions, how to evaluate results and how to ensure that the group process runs smoothly.

With its practical tone, its down-to-earth style and lively visuals, this is a book that will appeal strongly to managers and trainers looking for ways of improving their organization's and their department's performance.

Contents

1993   176 pages   0 566 07414 1 Hardback   0 566 07415 X Paperback

Gower